THE VOCAL COACH APPROACH

WHEN PRACTICE MAKES PERFECT

A guide to help singers of all levels learn to practice—and love it!

Susan Shiplett Ashbaker

THE VOCAL COACH APPROACH

WHEN PRACTICE MAKES PERFECT

A guide to help singers of all levels learn to practice—and love it!

Susan Shiplett Ashbaker

ISBN: 978-1-7335060-4-5

Inside View Press
Gahanna, Ohio

www.voxped.com

Printed in the United States of America

Edited by Scott McCoy

Dedication

With deepest gratitude to my mentors for their guidance along the way.

To Robert Mueller and Steven Barwick, my piano professors at Southern Illinois University, who believed in me and pushed me out of the nest in the best of all possible ways. To Mary Elaine Wallace at Southern Illinois University who turned my career choice around with the question, "Would you like to play for the opera this semester?" To John Wustman who smuggled me into many venues in Europe (during his concert tours with Luciano Pavarotti) for lessons, then shaped my role and ability as a vocal accompanist/coach at the University of Illinois. To Joan Dornemann who promised me the moon, then delivered it by sharing her Rolodex numbers with me and working with me in New York City and at the Metropolitan Opera when I had a grant from the National Institute for Music Theater. To Nico Castel and Robert (Bob) Cowart, who were picky with language and gave me a solid base from which to launch linguistically. And, finally to my beloved parents, Frances and Joe Shiplett, who were my first music teachers and gave me every opportunity they could think of to become a musician.

Thank you to Kyle St Sauveur for his assistance with the examples in Finale

THE VOCAL COACH APPROACH

TABLE OF CONTENTS

PART 2: DAILY NON-MUSICAL TOOLS

APPENDICES

Foreword: Support for Ashbaker's Work

The Vocal Coach Approach (When Practice Makes Perfect) by Susan Ashbaker joins a short, but distinguished list of books that should be considered essential for all who instruct and guide young performers of Opera and Art Song. It goes without saying that young singers can benefit greatly from listening to professionals who offer their experience and knowledge of performance traditions and communicate the information in an organized, logical manner. But good coaches who understand voices and vocal technique and have extensive knowledge of repertoire are very hard to find. Books written by professional voice coaches who can also share expertise in the intricacies of the business aspects of Classical Singing are fewer still.

In this book, Susan helps young singers work toward a synthesis of music, text, and style, utilizing all three of these components to fully enliven a character, a story line, and/or an event. Many young singers will never enjoy the benefits of working in person with a coach like Susan—one who has conducted operas, played piano reductions of opera scores, coached and accompanied for art song recitals, directed young artists' programs, and run entire opera companies. Drawn from a long and highly successful and productive career, Susan has skillfully distilled her knowledge into this handy *toolbox* for singers. The techniques and insights she shares will guide singers and their teachers as they tackle challenges of style, diction, and phrasing, and work toward a form of vocal expression that more faithfully reveals the intentions of both composer and poet. *The Vocal Coach Approach (When Practice Makes Perfect)* should be required reading for anyone wishing to be involved in the development of the next generation of great singers.

Christopher Arneson
Director of Voice Pedagogy, Westminster Choir College at Rider University

My longtime esteemed friend and colleague Susan Ashbaker has put together a most useful and practical set of techniques and methods for singers, vocal coaches, and other musicians to use in the study of music that they are learning and perfecting. In our field, she is widely admired for her honest and easy communication, and the ideas that are set forth here are exactly in that vein—they are simple to understand and quickly can be integrated into the habits of those persons who are unlocking the secrets of music as they improve their artistry. *Learning how to learn* is one of the most important skills anyone can develop. Such writing is a wonderful addition to the canon of thought and process for all of us, and I congratulate her on her accomplishment with this enlightening text!

Warren Jones
Pianist, Vocal Coach, and Conductor

Susan Ashbaker has worn many wonderful career hats in the many years I have known her. *The Vocal Coach Approach* combines these hats to share her practice ideas and strategies, which are vital to the growth of the singer's musical and performing abilities and enhance training with the voice teacher.

This diligent and detailed practice outline shows the singer how to pay close attention to details concerning the music, style of the composer, text, and communicating with the audience. Many singers are well disciplined, but it also takes curiosity, drive, patience, and perseverance when learning, practicing, and performing the music.

I believe this book is a wonderful addition to the voice studio library. Along with the voice teacher's guidance, it shows how diligent one must be with practice time and regimen. There is something for everyone in this book to learn or revisit, discuss, and pass on. The whole practice and learning routine never get old and it should never end throughout one's career. And yes, after 45 years I still find this truly rewarding and fun!

Sally Wolf
Voice Faculty, Westminster Choir College and Academy of Vocal Arts

Extraordinary performances are often described as "magical." Indeed, that is probably the most accurate description for those transporting experiences that defy the confines of language; but the nomenclature, however flattering, presents a dilemma for those who endeavor to become the delivery systems for making that kind of art. If "magical" is the result, then one might assume that the process is mystical, mysterious, or (even less helpful) just the result of a huge talent, or some ever elusive "it" factor. In truth, the "magic" we all seek is the result of work that has been enormously methodical. And this is where the brilliance of Susan Ashbaker steps it.

I have known Susan for much of my professional life, initially as a coach, producer, and assistant conductor, more recently, as a cherished co-teacher and collaborator. For several years, we led a series of workshops full of aspiring opera singers. Class after class we all marveled at her abilities to demystify the richly complicated processes of thorough preparation. At Susan's hand, these lucky young artists learned how to unearth, explore, develop, and ultimately inhabit the musical, textual and dramatic needs of any musical moment. Her methods are clear, concise, dependable, repeatable and (most importantly) fruitful!

I recommend this book to all who do, or teach, or simply aspire to understand. The kind of "magic" we all seek requires an egoless, humble, specific, and ordered process. Susan Ashbaker offers such a process… a method, indeed, for the magic.

Nova Thomas
Professor Voice, The Shepherd School of Music, Rice University
Teaching-Artist: Santa Fe Opera, Opera Theatre of St. Louis, Utah Opera, Palm Beach Opera

Introduction

Do you like to practice? If your answer is no, this book is for you! If your answer is yes, this book is for you, too! In the life of a singer, no matter what level, practice is the most significant portion of what you will be doing for those phenomenal hours in rehearsal and that glorious moment of performance.

What do *you* do when you practice? Let's start first with what it means to practice. According to Merriam-Webster it is, "to perform or work at repeatedly so as to become proficient, to train by repeated exercises, and systematic exercise of proficiency." So, practice includes repetition. But what happens if something goes wrong, and you repeatedly practice an error? That's right, you've practiced it perfectly wrong. Our repertoire is fraught with mistakes by the frequent practice of errors. That is why the idiom "practice makes perfect" is only possible if the practice is perfect[1]; otherwise, it will be perfectly incorrect. You need to have the right tools in place for practice, and your practice should include many tapas-sized portions of work.

In my home, I have a modest toolbox. The contents include a hammer, nails, and hardware for hanging pictures, a tape measure, a flat screwdriver, a Phillips screwdriver, and a set of very small screwdrivers. That is sufficient for what I do around my home. Everything else requires the expertise, interest, and toolbox of someone more skilled than I, whether it is re-grouting, putting up crown molding, renovating a bathroom, or building a closet.

As a singer, you need a professional-size toolbox for your craft; this book is just that. It can be read, reread, and regularly referenced. You can use the tools that will be most effective for you first, and then, as you integrate the skillsets into your practice, you can add more tools to your practice. This book is a lifelong study and is useful every time you learn a new piece or revisit a piece that is an old friend. It doesn't matter whether you are a freshman in college, have completed several young artist programs or are several years into a successful career. It doesn't matter if your chosen career path is as an opera singer, a choral singer, a music teacher, or a hobby musician. The exercises and ideas in the following chapters will help you learn to be more detailed and efficient with your time and in your practice and will show you multiple ways to get to a result you are amazingly proud of.

This book is the result of over 40 years of coaching singers. It is the result of the many teachers and mentors who taught me. It is the result of learning from the fabulous singers I've had the privilege of working with. It is the result of my love for finding ways to clarify concepts, provide particulars and help all singers become the very best possible version of themselves.

Susan Shiplett Ashbaker

---

1 "Perfect" is a curious word. According to the Merriam Webster Dictionary online, the definitions include "being entirely without fault or defect, flawless, satisfying all requirements, accurate, corresponding to an ideal standard or abstract concept… expert, proficient." In the arts, there are so many subjective opinions that "perfect" can be different for everyone. In this case, what can be right (satisfying all requirements) are the pitches, rhythms, and words. So, please proceed with caution, and don't let the word "perfect" stifle your artistic vision or creativity!

Part 1: Daily Musical Tools to Optimize Your Singing

Part 1.1

Everyday Tools for Musical Technique

If you are a serious student of singing, you likely begin your practice sessions by warming up your voice with exercises that your teacher has assigned. Like an athlete training for an event, these exercises are crucial for properly preparing your voice, body, and mind to work on your assigned repertoire. Some teachers also assign books of vocalises, such as *The Technics of Bel Canto* by Giovanni Battista Lamperti, *Practical Method of Italian Singing* by Nicola Vaccai, or *Bel Canto: A Theoretical and Practical Vocal Method* by Mathilde Marchesi. These volumes, among a great many others, are important to consider for your daily practice. But there's more you can do on your own!

I have identified five exercises for daily practice that are incredibly useful and can be applied to all repertoire (not just classical).

Before beginning, I ask you to close your eyes and touch your nose, and then touch your ears. I'm sure you were successful. How in the world did that happen when your eyes were closed? Well, you've been touching them your whole life. When you were fifteen months old, the adults in your life were thrilled if you got anywhere near your face when doing this, but now it is routine. The musical notes you must produce with your throat, body, and brain can become equally routine. These exercises will help you get there.

Pianists start practicing scales very early in their studies. Beginning with one hand, they gradually progress through playing two hands, extending the scales from one to two, or four octaves, in contrary motion, parallel thirds and sixths, and with varied rhythms and complexity. And then there is work to be done on arpeggios and various exercises by Czerny, Hanon, and multiple others. As skills develop, the pianist might move on to the incredibly difficult Chopin *Études,* highlighting very different skillsets in each of the *12 Études* of Opus 10, the *12 Études* of Opus 25 and three additional *Études* he wrote in 1839 (*étude* means study, a learning, practice, or preparation). Singers usually don't get this sort of progressive, systematic musical technique for their voice. Indeed, singers are different from pianists and other musicians; not only must they learn vocal technique, but they also are required to build their own instrument. Imagine if all instrumentalists had to spend the first few years in college building their violin, flute, or piano? Not so easy. Yet generation after generation of singers has risen to the occasion. I have the greatest respect for singers and everything they are required to do.

Process

Each day you identify your *pitch of the day* and *your vowel of the day*. Over the course of a year, you will have cycled through each pitch you sing in your range as well as all vowel sounds found in lyric singing (English, Italian, French, and German, at a minimum). For the following examples, we'll begin with C_4 (middle-C on the piano) and the vowel /i/. You can choose a metronome marking, if you like, as a reference for a consistent tempo; ♩ = 60 is a good starting point. Except for exercise five, I would not sing *with* the metronome. In these exercises, you need to find the center of the sound immediately so that you learn by doing, feeling exactly where the pitches are within you. It only takes five to ten minutes each day.

Tips

- Audio record your musical exercises frequently so that you can hear your work as immediate feedback to your actions.
- It might be helpful for you to create a chart for yourself of every pitch in your range and all the vowel sounds. Each day you can mark off the pitch and vowel you choose.

1. Half step whole step
   a. Begin on C and move upward a half step to C♯ on one measure of quarter notes, one of eighth notes and one of half note and half rest.
   b. Begin on C and move upward a whole step to D on one measure of quarter notes, one of eighth notes and one of half note and half rest.
   c. Begin on C and move downward a half step to B on one measure of quarter notes, one of eighth notes and one of half note and half rest.
   d. Begin on C and move downward a whole step to B♭ one measure of quarter notes, one of eighth notes and one of half note and half rest.

Figure 1: Half step, whole step exercises (vary the octave and starting pitch to fit your voice)

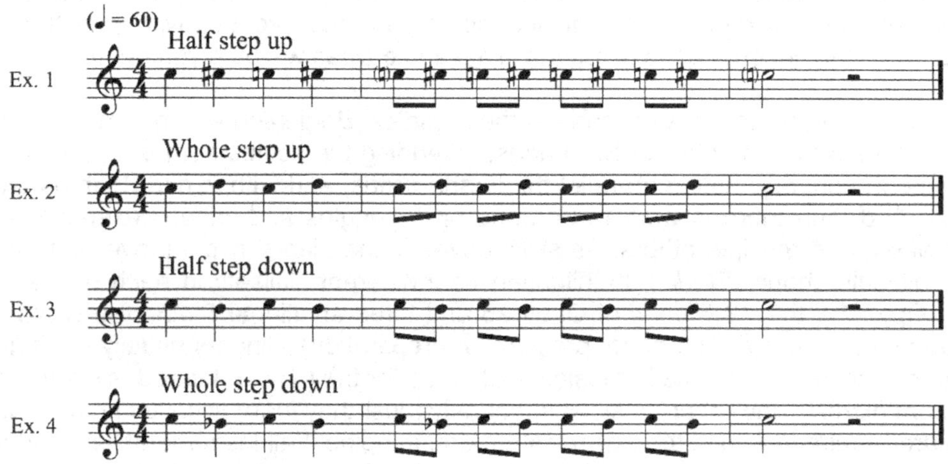

2. Scales
   a. Begin on C and sing a five-note **major** scale up and down, paying particular attention to singing in the center of the pitch
   b. If you are able, begin on C and sing a nine-note **major** scale up and down (to D), again paying particular attention to singing in the center of the pitch
   c. Once you have sung the five or nine note **major** scale, begin moving along the scale in an improvisatory manner. No skips are allowed. Tempo variations are encouraged once you know where the center of the sound is.

d. Begin on C and sing a five-note **minor** scale up and down, paying particular attention to singing in the center of the pitch. You can choose melodic or harmonic minor.
e. If you are able, begin on C and sing a nine-note **minor** scale up and down (to D), again paying particular attention to singing in the center of the pitch. Again, you can choose melodic or harmonic minor.
f. Once you have sung the five- or nine-note **minor** scale, begin moving along the scale in an improvisatory manner. No skips are allowed. Tempo variations are encouraged once you know where the center of the sound is.

Figure 2: Scales (practice from a variety of starting pitches)

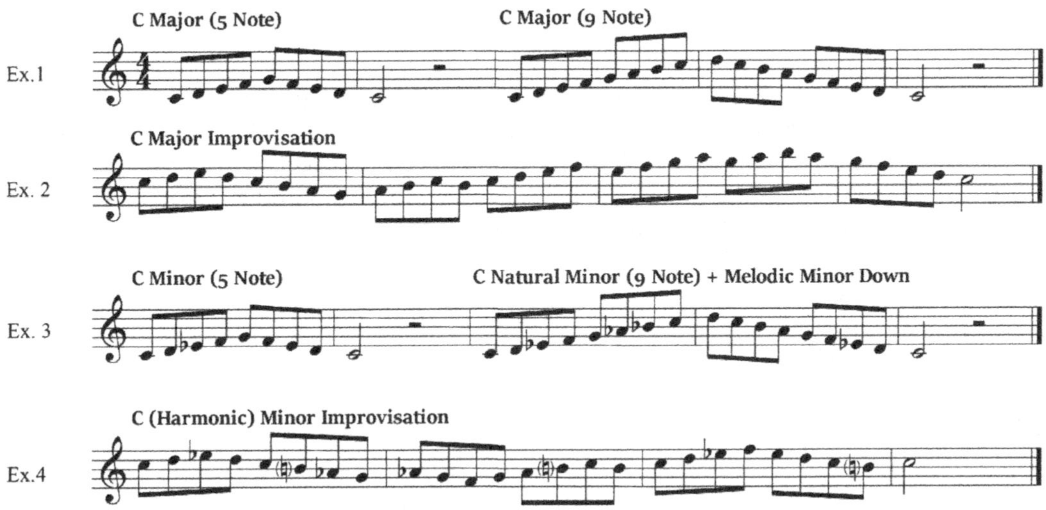

3. Arpeggio
    a. Begin on C and move forward on notes of equal value to E, G, C, G, E_4, C. (C-major arpeggio)
    b. Improvise on C, E, G throughout your range with skips of thirds fifths, octaves, and even a fourth down from C_4. Be gutsy on your arpeggios.
    c. Begin on C and move forward on notes of equal value to E♭,G, C, G, E♭, C. (C-minor arpeggio)
    d. Improvise on C, E♭, G throughout your range with skips of thirds, fifths, octaves, even a fourth down from C. Be gutsy on your arpeggios.
    e. After several months, add the seventh (raised and lowered on separate occasions)

Figure 3: Arpeggios and improvisation

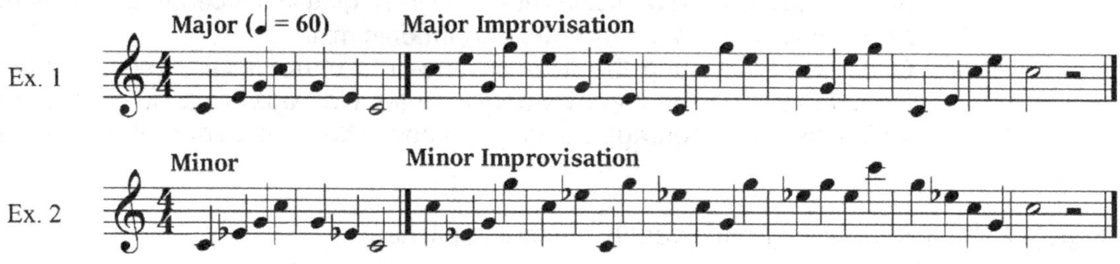

4. Trill
   a. The rhythm here is key: one measure of quarter notes, one of eighth notes, one of triplets, one of sixteenth notes, and trill. Be sure to STOP when you flat line (when the trill stops working) otherwise you will train your trill to always flat line at the end! You may breathe as needed except between the measures of sixteenth notes and trill.
   b. C to C♯
   c. C to D
   d. C to B
   e. C to B♭

Figure 4: Trills

5. *Messa di voce*
    a. Sing C on /i/
    b. Using a metronome marking of ♩ = 60, begin *pianissimo.* Over the count of three beats crescendo to *fortissimo* and then decrescendo over three beats back to *pianissimo.*
    c. Gradually extend this exercise to four, five, and ultimately ten beats

Figure 5: *Messa di voce*

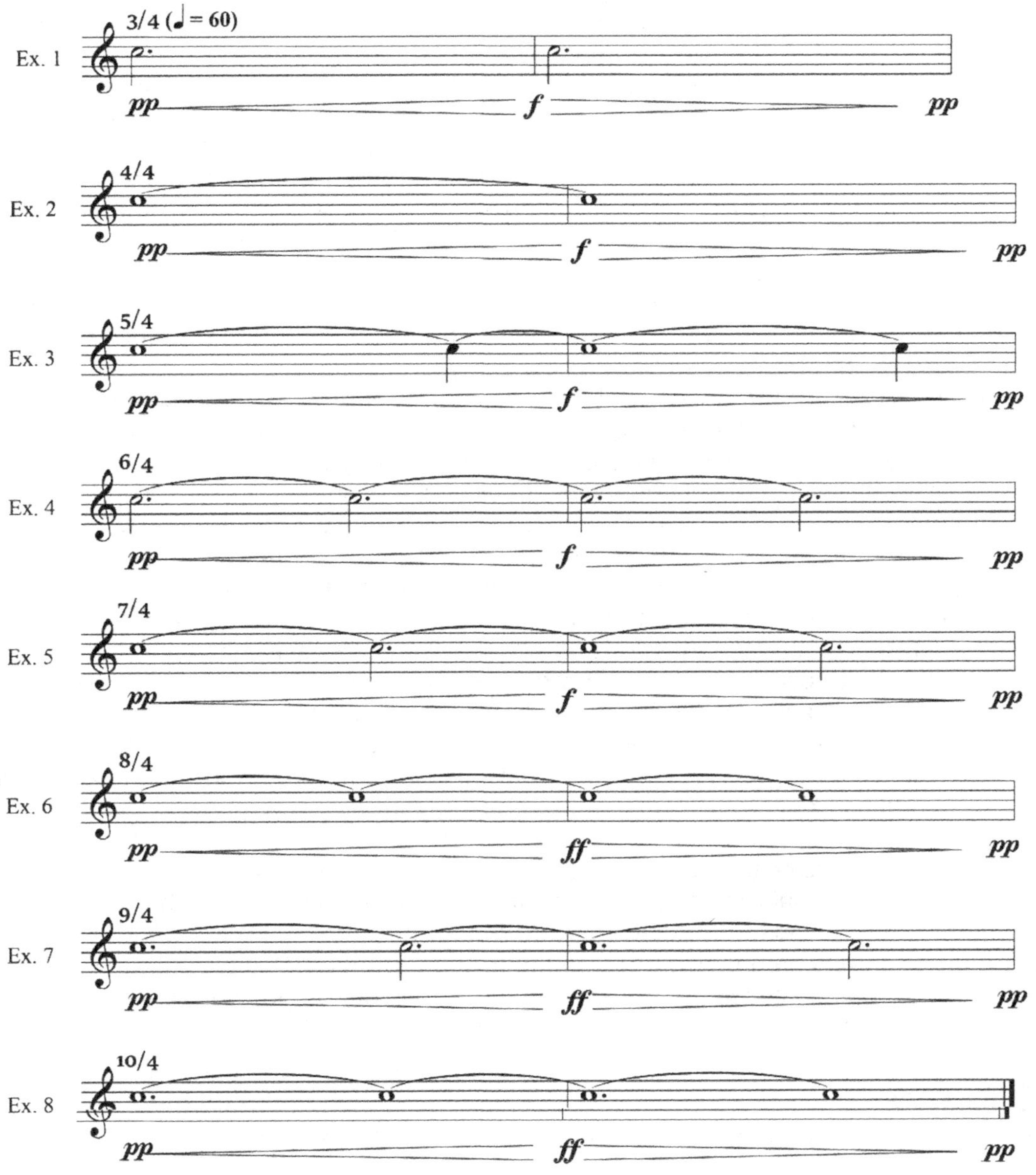

Variation

Once you are comfortable with Exercises 1, 2 and 3 you can vary the rhythms to shake it up a bit and create fun ways to continue this lifelong series of exercises. Learn to be comfortable with improvisation in this way and it will feel much easier to ornament your *da capo* arias.

Application to repertoire

1. Half steps and whole steps appear in every song, aria, or ensemble that you sing. Inexact placement of the pitch can throw an entire line flat or sharp. Learn to listen and feel for what is right for your voice.
2. Scales appear, either in whole or in part, in most songs, arias, or ensembles. Especially when the scales are rapid sixteenth notes, it can be intimidating. And frequently, the scales do not begin on the tonic, or *do* (as in do-re-mi), but if you've practiced the scales in this exercise, you will have improvised a variety of twists and turns so they are more approachable when you get to them in your repertoire. Scales frequently get sloppy when at a *vivace* tempo. By working on them daily, you maximize your chance for clarity.
3. Arpeggios are everywhere, and it is easy to hear intonation issues in them even with undiscerning ears. Practicing jumping around on arpeggio pitches will allow you to feel secure when you find them in your repertoire.
4. Trills are often dreaded, but it can be a learned skill. I must give credit to William Warfield, known affectionately by those who had the privilege of working with him as "Uncle Bill," for this exercise. He had an amazing trill, and he taught it this way. Whether approached from above or below, a measured trill over several beats or trill as a whole note, trills are here to stay. Please make friends with them.
5. *Messa di voce*, the crescendo/decrescendo of a tone while maintaining the integrity of the pitch, tone and color is one of the more difficult exercises. It's a bit like the swell pedal on the organ, which controls volume without adding or subtracting the various stops to change the color of the timbre. Getting to a crescendo over ten beats and a decrescendo over ten beats in one breath is a lifelong pursuit and you'll likely never achieve this on your highest and lowest tones. However, instead of dreading the final note of your piece that is held for eight beats plus a fermata, you will have the skill sets already in place to approach it with confidence.

These exercises are helpful and become more helpful over time when you have integrated them fully into your daily practice when singing or learning your music. "Aha, that is just a scale on sixteenth notes beginning on the fourth tone of the scale." "This is a minor arpeggio that skips around and ends on the raised seventh." "This pitch is sustained for eight beats but is preceded by two beats on other pitches. No problem, that's ten beats, or a five-to-five *messa di voce* exercise. I have breath for that."

Examples

Here are some examples of repertoire that clearly show the need for and application of these exercises.

Half step / whole step

Figure 6: "Ach, ich fühl's" from Mozart's *Die Zauberflöte*

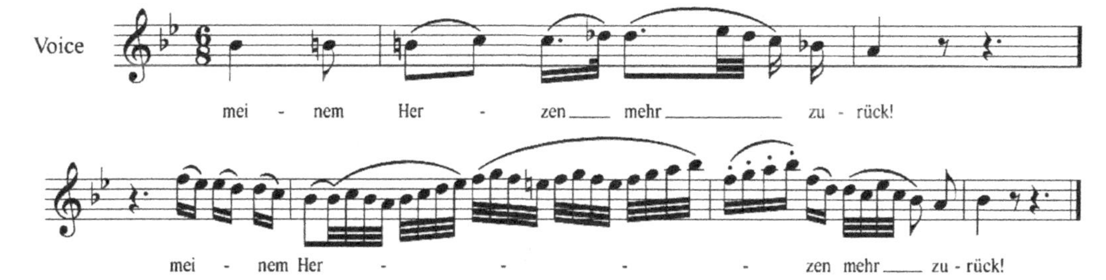

Figure 7: "Largo al factotum" from Rossini's *Il barbieri di Siviglia*

Figure 8: "Habanera" from Bizet's *Carmen*

Figure 9: "Je veux vivre" from Gounod's *Roméo et Juliette*

Scales

Figure 10: "Je veux vivre" from Gounod's *Roméo et Juliette*

Notice that the scale begins on the seventh, cueing a modulation to C major

Figure 11: "Mab" from Gounod's *Roméo et Juliette*

Figure 12: "Vous qui faites l'endormie" from Gounod's *Faust*

Figure 13: "Ich baue ganz" from Mozart's *Die Entführung aus dem Serail*

Figure 14: "Thus saith the Lord" from Handel's *Messiah*

Figure 15: "Nacqui all'affanno" from Rossini's *La Cenerentola*

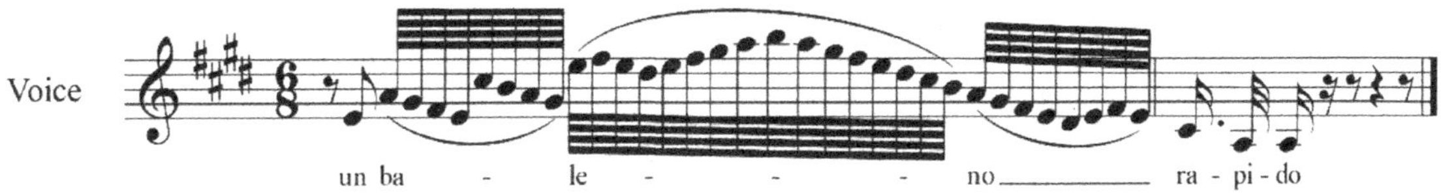

Arpeggio

Figure 16: "O wie ängstlich" opening from Mozart's *Die Entführung aus dem Serail*

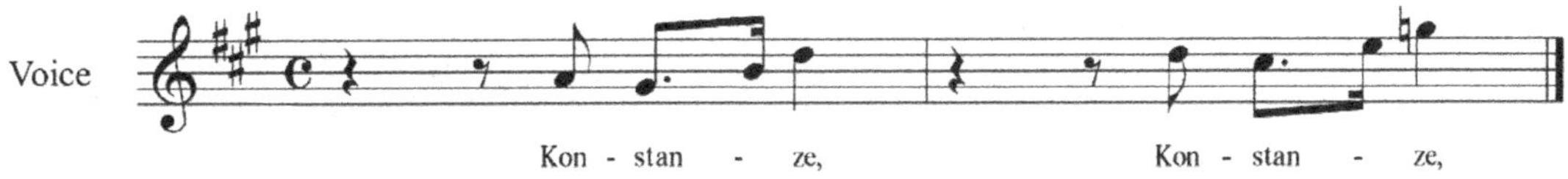

Figure 17 "Smanie implacabili" from Mozart's *Così fan tutte*

Figure 18: "Non più andrai" from Mozart's *Le nozze di Figaro*

Figure 19: "Deh, vieni non tardar" from Mozart's *Le nozze di Figaro*

Trill

Figure 20: "Ah, je ris" from Gounod's *Faust*

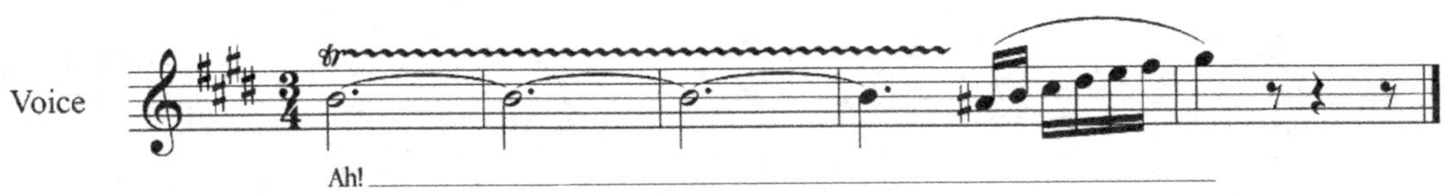

Figure 21: "Les oiseaux dans la charmille" from Offenbach's *Les contes d'Hoffman*

Figure 22: "O zittre nicht" from Mozart's *Die Zauberflöte* (measured trill)

Messa di voce

Figure 23: "Must the winter come so soon" from Barber's *Vanessa*

Figure 24: "Avant de quitter ces lieux" from Gounod's *Faust*

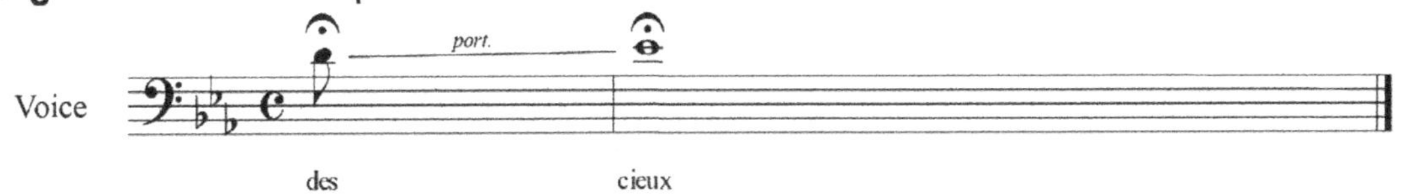

Figure 25: "Una furtiva lagrima" from Donizetti's *L'elisir d'amore*

Deconstructing repertoire for application of the five exercises

Figure 26: "O del mio dolce ardor" from Gluck's *Paride ed Elena*

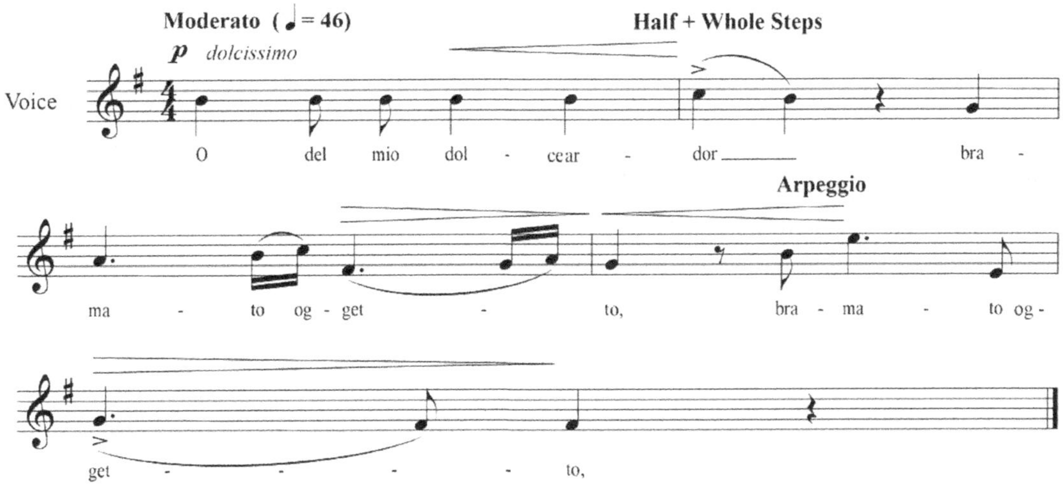

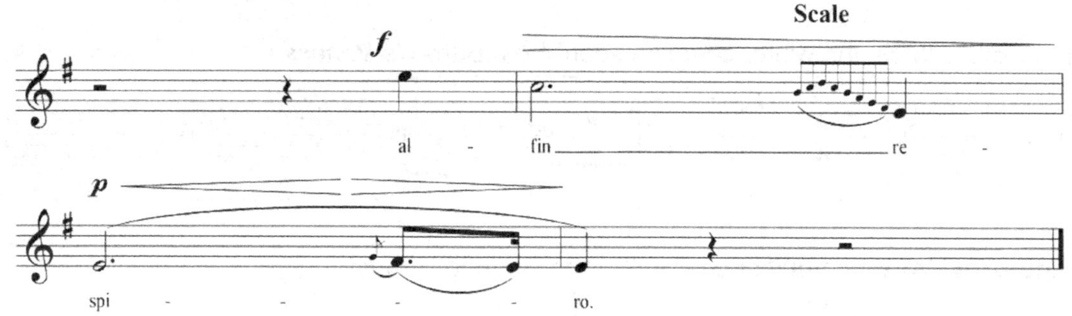

Figure 27: "Che fiero costume" from *Eteocle e Polinice* by Legrenzi

Figure 28: "Dies Bildnis ist bezaubernd schön" from Mozart's *Die Zauberflöte*

Figure 29: "Votre toast" from Bizet's *Carmen*

Figure 30: Excerpt from Olympia in Offenbach's *Les contes d'Hoffman*

Record your practice regularly

We are lucky to live at a time when recording capability is so easy. Let your phone, your tablet/iPad or computer serve you in the best possible way. When you are practicing, record your practice. Record the exercises above. Record everything you do vocally in the practice room. You need to feel what you are doing, but you also need feedback from a recording to see if you are accomplishing what you think you are as well as to hear the progress you have made.

Part 1.2

Words, Rhythms, and Pitches

In math, we learn that 2 + 2 = 4. We learn that all squares are rectangles, but not all rectangles are squares. There are certain absolutes. In music these absolutes are pitches, rhythms, and words. They are either right, or they are wrong. Let's first look at the words.

Words

Composers choose specific words to be set to music, written by poets, librettists, or themselves. In most instances, they are fluent in the language in which they write—if not native speakers—and take great care to make the music fit the words. Unless you are singing a translated version of the text, it is highly unlikely that once you learn these words you will need to master a different set of words for the same music years later (at least from a reputable publisher or score), so it is important to honor the words of those who wrote them as well as those who set them to music. Made up words don't count. There are more details in *Part 2: Daily Non-Musical Tools*, that will help you feel comfortable with the text. But you MUST sing the correct words.

Rhythms

The composer, whom we've established is either native or fluent in the language of the selection, had a multitude of choices as to how to set the text. The words were set in a particular rhythm based on the concept of the composer and the understanding of how that word works with the musical ideas in the composition, so make sure to learn the rhythms correctly from the start. Begin with rhythm alone, waiting to add the words after the rhythms are mastered. This is work that can be done in a small speaking voice, provided the words and rhythms are correct. Muscle memory will want to keep it where you first put it. So good or bad, right, or wrong, it is there. The rhythms MUST be right.

Pitches

Again, the composer had a multitude of choices in deciding which pitch was paired with which word and rhythm. Most composers are inspired by the text to create a feeling in tandem with the emotion they are looking for in their composition; we owe them accuracy and must honor their vision. Beyond that, people who sit on audition panels and make decisions, almost certainly know the music you are singing as well as, and probably better than you. They will know if you sing a pitch or rhythm incorrectly. If you have sufficient piano skills to play your pitches and rhythms correctly, that's terrific. Listening to recordings is also helpful (although many recordings, even of great artists, have musical errors in them). Your pianist can also record your pitches in the correct rhythms so you can listen and integrate both. I wouldn't recommend singing full voice to a recording like this. But you certainly can track the rhythms and pitches by marking (singing lightly). It often is helpful to deconstruct the harmonic structure so that you know where you are in relation to the harmony. Don't panic, this is not a book on theory, rather a helpful tool for new music, Strauss, Wagner, or other composers who have challenging harmonies. Find the harmonic bones of your selection. Where does your vocal line fit in? Who changes harmony first, you, the orchestra, the piano? Does your pitch fit into a triad? Is it an appoggiatura or a passing tone? How the pitches function informs what you can do musically.

Figure 31: “Sein wir wieder gut!” from Strauss’s *Ariadne auf Naxos*

In Part 3, several common mistakes will be clarified in repertoire for each voice type. This is your opportunity to be a music sleuth so that you can detect correct pitches, rhythms, and words.

Part 1.3

Working on Meter, Tempo, Rhythm, and Clarity

Rhythms for practice

So, you've opened a new piece and all you see is measure after measure of sixteenth notes. Likely, your heart rate speeds up a bit. How in the world do you learn this, and how do you sing it at tempo?

As a pianist, I learned early on that in fast passages filled with sixteenth notes (or 32nd notes, or even 64th notes!) a variety of rhythms helped with fluency. If you practice slowly and correctly, that doesn't necessarily mean that you will be able to play it correctly *a tempo.* There are four basic rhythms to use, as evidenced by the examples below

Figure 32: Rhythms for Practice

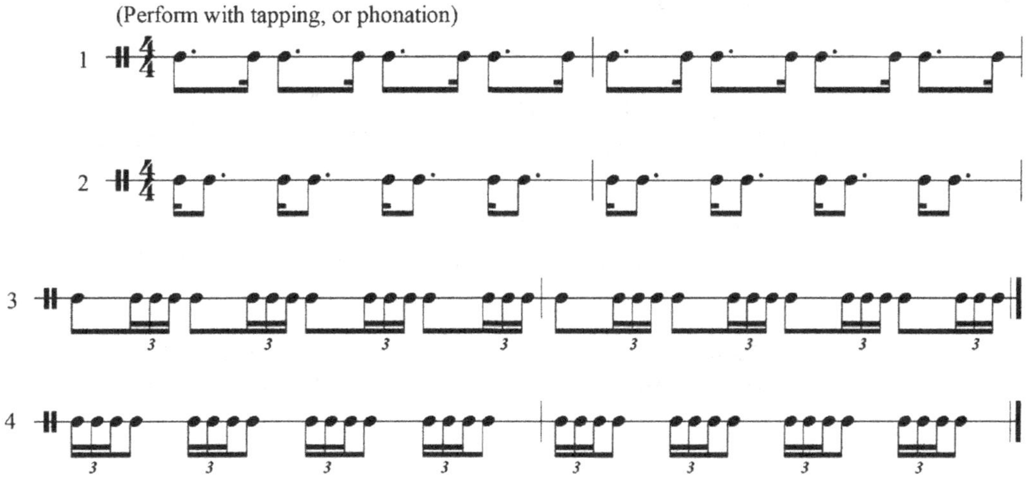

In the early part of my career, I had the great fortune to be the graduate assistant to *Kammersängerin* Teresa Stich-Randall at Southern Illinois University's Marjorie Lawrence Opera Theater. In listening to her recordings, I was especially drawn to her clarity and velocity. I asked her how she practiced to be able to produce such extraordinary singing and was astonished to hear that she used the practice rhythms that I, as a pianist, had learned. As a singer, you must be careful not to overdo it with enthusiasm. It is intensive work and demands your full vocal and mental attention.

Figure 33: Eight-measure Excerpt, “O zittre nicht” from Mozart’s *Die Zauberflöte*

Using the example above, here’s how you would approach this rhythmic exercise. First, break it down into small segments (I like to call it “tapas sized” segments). It is usually five sixteenth notes; the four sixteenths in the first beat and the first sixteenth note in the second beat. By doing this as a practice, you are constantly building a bridge to the next set of notes.

Figure 34: Five-note groupings applied to “O Zittre nicht”

Once you are comfortable with the groupings of five, you may go to groupings of seven and then nine. Once that is comfortable, you can go to eleven, thirteen, or even longer segments. At each practice session, begin with a different beat as your starting location.

Variations on this practice include starting on the third sixteenth note of a beat and singing the group of five. This takes a great deal of concentration. But the result is that you truly know the notes in the passage.

Figure 35: Variations on five-note segments

II 

III 

IV 

These exercises should be done at varying, but consistent tempi. Start slowly for clarity but vary the tempo. You'll notice that even at the slow tempo, the rhythms give you the opportunity to move quickly, but have a place to pause to keep your bearings.

Triplets

There are two ways to approach triplets.

1. To find the backbone, simply sing the first note of each triplet. Practice in this manner several times so that the backbone is clear. Review the Everyday Tools For Musical Technique to help identify what the structure is and which tools you can use for your practice.
2. Most of your time, however, will be spent on the middle note of the triplet. This is the note that frequently becomes what I like to call an "X" note. An X note is any note that, upon hearing, is impossible to write down or identify in music dictation. (This also happens frequently with the sixteenth note in dotted rhythms.) You've worked so hard to develop your beautiful sound. Don't throw it away by singing X notes!

To practice this middle pitch, there are two techniques I encourage.

1. First, sing the triplet with an accent on the middle note. Do this first at a slower tempo to ensure precise intonation, then increase the tempo.

2. The second tool is to shift the rhythm to sixteenth notes and sing the middle note of the triplet as two sixteenth notes. Again, first at a slower tempo, then speeding up.

Figure 36: Triplets and core melodic structure
Mozart, "Hai già vinta la causa" *Le nozze di Figaro*

Figure 37: Triplets with accents
Mozart "Parto, parto, ma tu, ben mio" *La clemenza di Tito*

Figure 38: Original with accents and rhythmic variations
Mozart "Come Scoglio" *Così fan tutte*

Four Note Groupings (♩ = 60)

Seven Note Groupings (♩ = 60)

Even when you have succeeded in singing a clear triplet passage, occasionally pull out this practice tool to keep your precision intact!

Changing tempi and shifting meters

Why is it often so hard to change tempi or shift meters? Unless it is clearly marked and rather intuitive, it is necessary to do some further looking. Finding the least common denominator often helps with this transition. What do I mean by that?

EXAMPLE 1 (Beethoven, "O wär ich schon" *Fidelio*)
In this example, the common denominator is the eighth note. If you pay attention to the subdivision, you will be able to track the change with ease.

Figure 39: Excerpt from Beethoven "O wär ich schon" *Fidelio*

EXAMPLE 2 (Britten, *Peter Grimes*)

In this example, the common denominator is also the eighth note, but from a different perspective. Written with the ♪ = 112, which translates roughly to the ♩. = 37, singers and pianists can move with ease from the various rhythms if they use the perspective of the dotted quarter note. In the 2/4 measures the time continues but goes from a triple to a duple feeling. In the second example, the two singers with quarter notes can use the ♪ = 112 as their rhythmic compass while the other singer and pianist can keep it in a broad two-beat pattern.

Figure 40: Excerpt from Britten *Peter Grimes*

Part 1.4

Vowels, Vocal Colors, and Expressivity

Know your best vowel

I'm often surprised when I ask singers, "What is your best vowel," and they are perplexed! You are the expert in your voice. When you are working on a challenging passage, choose your BEST vowel for the work. Some vowels work better than others, depending upon the pitch and range in your voice, so finding your best vowel must be a priority for you. It shouldn't take too long and is a good conversation to have with your voice teacher so that you have guidance when working on passages using only a vowel. Once you are clearly in charge of the passage, you can migrate your vowel to the correct vowels of the phrase. This will help you with vocal color and consistency and allow for your unique expressivity.

Work with colors

When playing with your melodic lines on your best vowel, it is also terrific to work with colors. Yes, actual colors. We frequently associate colors with various moods. Think about your feelings of color in your clothing, your furniture, your curtains, and your walls. Many people associate red with anger and yellow with happiness; however, what is most important here is what the colors mean specifically to YOU. Thinking about specific colors while you sing can influence the tone-color (timbre) of your voice. If it is difficult for you to imagine colors, make 3x5 flash cards with all the colors you can think of, or consult a color chart or color wheel online. For example, you might write *green* on a card, or more specifically, *olive* green, *lime* green, or even *sea foam* green. "Shades of blue" put into your browser will give you a wide variety of choices in blue, as will every other color you input. You can even buy a box of colored pencils or crayons and physically color your 3x5 card. Your own creativity will help you find what works best for you and will give you a complete palette of colors and timbres from which to work.

Cards for emotions

I wish I had thought to invest in 3x5 card stock years ago. I use them all the time, and I suggest you do the same. In addition to your color cards or online sources. I encourage you to have three- to five hundred flash cards with various adjectives, adverbs, and states of being. This is helpful when working on text alone, when working with one vowel, and when integrating text and music together.

The internet can also work here as well, if you prefer. Look up words of emotion or action in the thesaurus and you'll have a long list with which to work. You can put these words on a document and pull them up when you are practicing.

With text, you can use all your flash cards. Choose a short portion of your text, for example *Quando me'n vo soletta per la via* from Puccini's *La bohème.* (More detailed text work is included in Part 2.) Pull a card and speak the phrase in that attitude. Pull another card and change attitudes. You can have lots of fun with this. And, when you add "attitude," your language skills usually improve.

When you move to singing a phrase or a section, such as the first sixteen measures of "Quando me'n vo," you pull from your set of cards ten to twenty cards that fit the scenario.

Examples for this could include confident, charming, desire, beauty, sexy, fiery, proud, coquettish, or risqué, just to name a few. You can use a card for the entire section or pull cards as you wish. Either approach gives you specific direction in exploring the vocal colors of your Musetta and what she's saying (as well as what she's not saying!). This technique can help you find the expression in the language as you deepen your understanding of the character you are portraying.

A cappella work

Why a cappella work? It is important to work without any accompaniment so that you truly can hear what you are doing. There is nothing to hide behind. Don't be shy—you need to find the essence of what you are doing. Are your colors and intentions clear? Is your language accurate and clear? Are you singing with line and legato? Are you in tune? Record yourself frequently when you practice.

Caution! Often, singers skip over the rests, migrate the pitch flat or sharp, or lose the rhythmic integrity when working a cappella. If you are practicing a cue-to-cue, ignoring the rests can work. But too often, singers forget the actual duration of the rests. So, practice a cappella while paying strict attention to the rests as well. Use a metronome to help keep yourself rhythmically honest, and don't presume that the accompaniment will make it clear for you. You need to know exactly the length of your rests and the details in your rhythm. For pitch accuracy, playing a chord once every measure or two can help you stay in tune. Recording your a cappella work and listening back is also helpful. Make sure you look at the pitches, rhythms, and rests carefully when listening to your recording.

Line and legato

My teacher, John Wustman, always would say "Legato is a way of life." He is right. While the concept might be challenging at first, once you know how to sing legato, it IS a way of life. However, I divide line and legato into two separate categories.

Legato comes from the Italian verb, *legare*, which means to connect, bind, or tie. What is it that we are binding, connecting, or tying together? Mr. Wustman had a specific answer for that as well, that I have incorporated into my coaching as well. We are binding together SOUND. Vowel sounds, consonant sounds, all sounds.

Line, for me, is a vocal GPS. It tells me where you are going musically.

You can have line without legato. You can have legato without line. But when you have legato and line, then you can take your listener on a musical journey. Legato functions much like the fluidity of a wonderful conductor. There are few surprises with a seasoned conductor; everything they want is in their gesture. Everything for you, the singer, is in your breath, legato, and line.

Part 1.5

Fixing Places That Were Learned Wrong

It is commonly believed that bad habits are easier to acquire than to break. Indeed, I used to believe that breaking a habit took at least twice as long as creating it. But conventional wisdom suggests that the time frame is the same, as breaking a *bad* habit is just forming a *new* habit. But it's hard to let go of a bad habit, which is why it is helpful to have a *replacement* behavior available, as well as some strong motivation.

Specifically, I would tell singers that it takes about 27 repetitions to form a habit and 66 to break it. So, I would ask them to practice their new (corrected) way 100 times in a row (that day or over the course of several days) accurately, and they'd have it fixed. This was usually referencing a wrong rhythm, text, or pitch.

That is both true and false. Let's investigate why.

The adage was that it takes about 21 days to create a habit. This likely began in the 1950s with Maxwell Maltz, a surgeon, who noticed that it took him and others about 21 days to adapt to a changed habit or look (in the surgical field, plastic surgery). His self-help book "Psycho Cybernetics, A New Way to Get More Living Out of Life," offers details of his research and experience. But the idea of "21 days to form a habit" is a huge misrepresentation that provoked many presumptions and mythical thinking. (Maltz, Maxwell. *Psycho-Cybernetics.* New York, NY, Simon & Schuster, 1960.)

An article by James Clear cites a follow-up study conducted by Philippa Lally, a health psychology researcher, on this topic. Per the study a new habit takes 66 days to form, with as many as 254 days until it is more securely formed[2].

You can find a great deal of useful information online. Here are two articles to get you started.

> https://www.forbes.com/sites/jasonselk/2013/04/15/habit-formation-the-21-day-myth/#32ceb4b8debc
>
> https://www.capespace.com/how-the-21-90-rule-helps-you-build-good-habits-and-a-better-life/

But this section of the book is not about the data of habit forming and breaking, even though it is a fascinating topic; it is about the practical application of habit forming and habit breaking related to singing. The reality is that what works for one person doesn't necessarily work for another. Some habits may be easier to make or break, such as those regarding text, pitches, or rhythms, while technical habits to make or break can take quite a bit of time. There is no magic number; there is never a Cinderella (*Cenerentola,*

---

[2] Clear, James. (April 10, 2014) *How Long Does It Actually Take to Form a New Habit? (Backed by Science). The Huffington Post.* Blog. https://www.huffpost.com/entry/forming-new-habits_b_5104807

Cendrillon) moment when the clock chimes and your life is suddenly transformed by your habit, nor does a Fairy Godmother (with assistance from the forest animals) do the work for you. It takes persistence, diligence, and focus.

Making a habit

Building good habits is part of the practice paradigm. The more you do something, the more easily it becomes a habit. Take the time, in early learning, to focus clearly so that what you learn is correct.

Some habits are easy to form and are prompted by actions, such as buckling your seatbelt when you get into a car or brushing your teeth before you go to bed. Determine which easily formed habits you can make part of your practice routine. Perhaps it is the five exercises referenced in Part 1.1 *Everyday Tools For Musical Technique*. Perhaps it is your preparatory breath before beginning a phrase. Perhaps it is your warm-up routine each day.

Working too fast without focus and concentration can develop bad habits, which are then difficult to break. Let this be a cautionary tale.

Be attentive in the beginning of habit forming to work in smaller sections. As mentioned earlier, I like to call this tapas-sized practice bites. Your body and voice don't know what is right and wrong technically or musically, just what you tell it to do most often. So, make sure you are fully alert and that you serve the technique you've worked so hard to achieve.

Example 1: from "Ach, ich fühl's" by Mozart, *Die Zauberflöte*

- *Ach*—the placement of the vowel
    - Find your best vowel first and play around with the best dynamic in that vowel
    - Then sing your best vowel and migrate the vowel to the A
    - This helps ensure that your first pitch is well placed
- *fühl's*—the *appoggiatura*
    - Sing the first five tones of the g minor scale very carefully up and down the scale to ensure proper placement and consistent sound. This can be done on the vowel of the word *fühl's*
    - sing *re* and *do* only, leaning into the *re* (movable *do*)
- Octave skip on *es ist*
    - Using your "comfort" vowel (aka your best vowel), sing the high g several times
    - Once the g is secure, use a *portamento* to find your way to the lower g
    - Now sing the G_5 to the G_4 without the actual *portamento,* just thinking it. Work for the consistency of the sound like you achieved in the exercise with the *portamento*
    - Repeat these steps using the vowels of the words in the aria
- *verschwunden*—the *appoggiatura*
    - Sing the last four tones of the G minor scale very carefully beginning on *do* to ensure proper placement and consistent sound. This can be done on your comfort vowel.
    - Repeat this exercise using the vowel u or U

- Sing *la* and *sol* only (E♭ to D), leaning into the *la* (the appoggiatura)

- Put it all together, paying careful attention to consistent and beautiful sound with terrific intonation. You have now created a habit that you need to reinforce for the beginning of your aria.

Figure 41: Opening phrase of "Ach, ich fühl's" from Mozart's *Die Zauberflöte*

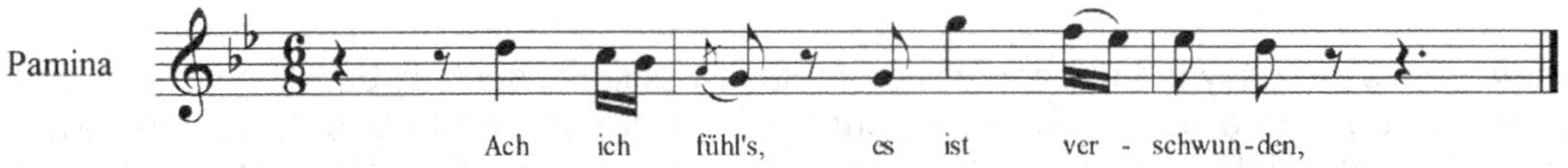

Breaking a habit

As the song says, "Breaking up is hard to do." But you do need to break up with your bad habits.

How do you change a habit? First, you need to know that a problem exists. This usually happens when your teacher or coach points out the problem; however, you won't be able to change it until you recognize it yourself. Once you hear or feel the issue, you can take steps to change the behavior.

If it is a rhythm mistake, break it down so that you understand the rhythm to be corrected. What is the correct rhythm? What were you doing? What do you need to do to fix the rhythm?

Example 2: From "Zueignung" by Richard Strauss

- This is a classic case of duple versus triple. The orchestra has a strong triplet figure throughout the song. The voice comes in with a duple rhythm. You need to correct your eighth note because you are singing it as a triplet.
- With text only, and clapping or tapping eighth notes, speak the correct rhythm of the first two measures, *Ja, du weisst es, teure Seele*, ten or more times
- With pitches or text, only on your best vowel with a consonant attached (e.g. /lo/), clap or tap eighth notes and sing the correct rhythm of the first two measures, ten or more times
- Integrate your learning by singing the correct text on the correct pitches in the correct rhythm, continuing to tap or clap, ten or more times
- Sing the same two measures only tapping or clapping on the quarter notes, ten or more times
- Repeat with the pianist playing chords as eighth notes
- Repeat with the pianist playing chords as quarter notes
- Repeat with the pianist playing the triplets on beats one, three and four.
- Repeat with the pianist playing the accompaniment as written

Figure 42: Excerpt from "Zueignung" by Richard Strauss

Original

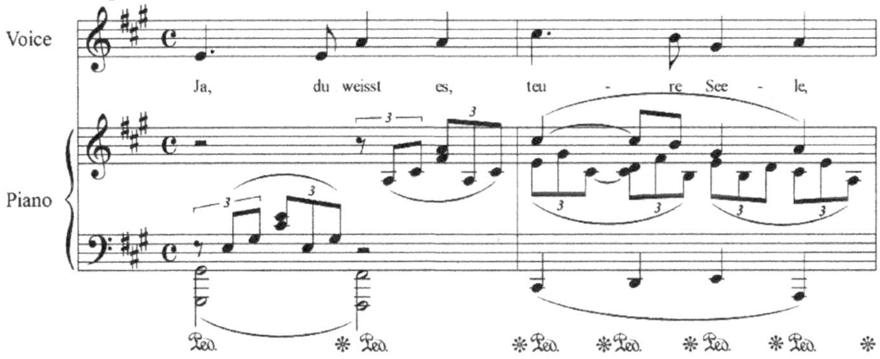

Block Chords in Eighth Notes

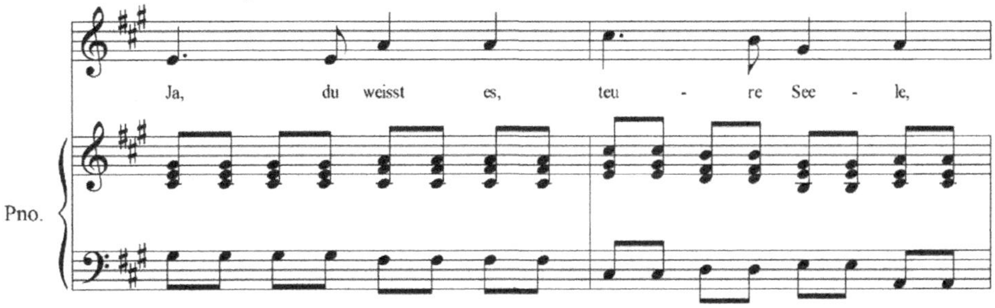

Same Chords, but in Quarter Notes

Accompaniment as written, but every second beat has a Quarter Note Chord

Oops… I forgot

If you forget to continue your habit-forming practice, don't despair, just jump back on the bandwagon. If it was only a day or two, it will be easier to get back into the groove of forming good habits. Go back to whichever practice step you feel you need. If you go back to step one, you will likely be able to advance more quickly than the first time. However, this is not a race. Once you have a system that works for you, the time needed to create good habits and break bad habits will likely shorten.

Part 1.6

Learning To Keep Your Sound Consistent

I don't want to discourage you, but keeping your sound consistent is a lifelong process. As a vocal athlete, your sound will change as you age and your body changes. It is crucial to have a unified, focused, and consistent sound. Technique is first and foremost, so talk to your teacher frequently about this. If something in this book does not align with your teacher's process, please *listen to your teacher*. You are paying them to build your vocal technique, while I am here to help you practice efficiently, smartly, and well.

What I offer here are exercises to help you find consistency with a variety of musical suggestions. As in all exercises in this book, don't overdo the idea!!! Tapas sized practice bites are best.

Lip Trills and Tongue Trills

Singing your phrases on a lip trill or tongue trill will offer you the opportunity to keep your breath graded and evenly dispersed as you sing through the phrases. This exercise and the repetition of it helps you build the best practice habit of taking the right breath and keeping the support evenly distributed.

Comfort Vowel

It is important to know what your comfort vowel is, or what your favorite vowel is. Everyone has one, and it usually is not AH! If you are not sure, ask your teacher and coach what they think. Or, better yet, experiment so that you know for sure what your best vowel is. Note that your favorite vowel, or comfort vowel, may change over time and likely is not the same throughout your singing range.

Once you have identified your comfort vowel, sing phrases on that vowel. Record your singing. Listen to the recording. Note how it feels. Ultimately, you will need to accurately self-assess whether your sound is consistent. Of course, your teacher and coach can help you, but they are not in the practice room with you daily. This is the opportunity to get real with yourself.

Over time, singing all your phrases on your comfort vowel will help you with your consistency in a way that will integrate with how you first approach a new piece.

How to navigate the high pitches in your phrase

So often, singers focus on the first pitch they are to sing, which often ends up being short sighted. It is crucial to look at the highest pitch in that phrase and gauge your first note on that note, otherwise, it is a perpetual uphill battle.

EXAMPLE 1: "Dies Bildnis" from Mozart's *Die Zauberflöte*

- Sing the G_4 first on your comfort vowel
- Sing the G_4 on your comfort vowel, and then sing the $B\flat_3$ (always legato)
- Repeat Example 2 singing G_4, $B\flat_3$, and then G_4

- Sing an E♭ major scale up to the G_4 and back in a thoughtful and focused way
- Sing your G_4 on your comfort vowel and sing the descending scale as written to the $A\flat_3$.
- Repeat Examples 1-5 on the vowels of the aria, singing the G_4 first on your comfort vowel
- Repeat Examples 1-5 on the text, singing the G_4 first on your comfort vowel
- Record this process so that you can listen to your sound as well as the integrity and beauty of your high pitch as well as all others

Figure 43: "Dies Bildnis" from Mozart's *Die Zauberflöte*

Intonation

If you have been focusing on the five exercises in Part 1.1, your intonation already should be better. When coaching singers, I work with them to determine if they are aware of their intonation issues; they often will identify the problem as lack of support, the wrong kind of support, or over-singing. When intonation is an issue, singers often have lost their physical and vocal grounding. There can also be the issue of focus of sound that results in singers being either high or low on the pitch. Not utilizing the overtones in the sound can pull the pitch down, and losing focus and support can also cause the sound to spread into a wider or whiter, often breathier sound.

Portamenti

Portamenti are terrific as a practice tool. The word *portamento* is from the Italian verb *portare,* which means to carry. In singing, you are carrying the sound, either up or down. Using a *portamento* between two pitches can give you an easier way to get there. In practice you can do this on any repertoire as a tool, and I encourage you to do it often

EXAMPLE: "Deh vieni, non tardar" from Mozart's *Le nozze di Figaro*

- Without rhythm, simply sing the first five notes of the aria on your comfort vowel with a big *portamento* between each pitch (C_5, F_5, A_4, C_5, F_4). (Again this shows you how crucial and useful the arpeggio exercise in Part 1.2 is!)
- Repeat Example 1 with the vowels of the text
- Repeat Example 1 with the text
- Sing the text with *portamenti* in rhythm
- Sing the text without *portamenti* in rhythm (think the *portamenti,* however)

Figure 44 "Deh vieni, non tardar" from Mozart's *Le nozze di Figaro*

Ends of long phrases

EXAMPLE: "Sul fil" from Verdi's *Falstaff*
(Presuming a breath after the word *hanno*)

1. Sing the A_5 on the word *fior* for as long as you can, reinforcing this by doing it multiple times over several days
2. Sing the G♯ on the text *fre i* and the A on the word *fior,* again holding the A_5 for as long as you can, reinforcing this by doing it multiple times over several days
3. Back up one quarter note to the G♮ and sing the end phrase, again holding the A5 for as long as you can, reinforcing this by doing it multiple times over several days
4. Back up one quarter note to the F♯ and sing the end phrase, again holding the A_5 for as long as you can, reinforcing this by doing it multiple times over several days
5. Back up one quarter note to the E♮ and sing the end phrase, again holding the A_5 for as long as you can, reinforcing this by doing it multiple times over several days
6. Back up to the sixteenth note D♯ and sing the end phrase, again holding the A_5 for as long as you can, reinforcing this by doing it multiple times over several days
7. Sing the phrase from the beginning, *Le Fate hanno,* stopping when you need a breath, reinforcing this by doing it multiple times over several days

8. Sing the phrase from the beginning, *Le Fate hanno,* with a larger than normal breath after the word *hanno* (don't worry about how long it takes you to get a good breath, in this exercise just take the time), reinforcing this by doing it multiple times over several days
9. Sing the phrase from the beginning, *Le Fate hanno,* taking a breath about half the size of the breath after the word *hanno*, reinforcing this by doing it multiple times over several days
10. Sing the phrase from the beginning, *Le Fate hanno,* halving the size of the breath once more after the word *hanno*, reinforcing this by doing it multiple times over several days
11. Sing the phrase from the beginning, *Le Fate hanno*, taking a normal breath after the word *hanno* for rhythmic and musical integrity and finish the phrase
12. You will now have a clearer idea of the kind of breath you need and strategies for success in the phrase

Figure 45: "Sul fil" from Verdi's *Falstaff*

Should you choose to sing from *Le Fate hanno per cifre* then breathe and sing *i fior*, the practice strategy is still the same. You and your teacher can decide which breath option is best for you now.

Home stretch

I find the best way to practice the final stretch of any aria is to practice it when you are fresh and warmed up. If you have made a routine of singing the final sixteen measures or so of your aria when you are in wonderful voice, then your voice will have an easier time of finding (and remembering) the way at the end of the aria when you have started from the beginning (or when it is at the end of the second or third aria you are asked to sing). If you leave the final measures until the end to practice, your voice will remember to be fatigued and tired each time. And your hard work for a consistent sound will disappear. Your body/voice does not always know right from wrong, just what you have it do time after time. Practice for success in the home stretch.

Part 1.7

Learning Recitative

Recitative. What does that word mean? It comes from the Italian verb *recitare,* which means to recite, declaim, or say aloud. The text almost always is more important than the melody in recitative. *Encyclopedia Britannica* has the following definition: "Recitative, style of monody (accompanied solo song) that emphasizes and indeed imitates the rhythms and accents of spoken language, rather than melody or musical motives."

To do this successfully, you must have an intimate knowledge of the words, their sounds, and their meanings. There should be a natural inflection of the speech pattern in whatever language the recitative (shortened frequently to *recit*) is. It usually carries the action from an aria or ensemble or chorus, to another aria, ensemble, or chorus. It moves the plot along. A google search regarding recitatives will bring up a variety of books from which you can choose, depending upon the type of recitative you are undertaking. Or visit a music library either in person or online, where you will be able to find resources to address your current recitative questions. I encourage you to find out as much as you can about this specific area of singing.

In this section, you'll gain a variety of tools on how to look at your recitatives and how to practice them so that you sound fluent. A reminder that even though these practice tips will be helpful, you will need to approach every recitative you sing in a stylistically correct manner. Be sure to look at the name of the composer and the era in which it was written before you begin studying a recitative (recitatives by Bach are very different from those by Verdi). Listening to professional singers sing recitative is a great learning tool as well.

Speed

In spoken conversation, each person has a particular way of speaking; some people speak faster and some slower, while others speak at a higher or lower pitch. In conversation, it is normal for us to infuse emotion into what we are talking about. Sometimes we speak quickly and other times more slowly. Usually, these conversations are about our own lives, our opinions, and our thoughts, so we are often very passionate about things. We have these conversations authentically. We don't have to think, "Shall I say this in an excited way?" We just let our genuine selves take over.

This is exactly what you need to do in recitative, so the first thing to do is to translate. You need to know the depths of the words that you will be singing. A translation template is included in the Appendix at the end of the book.

Once you are confident with your translation you need to create a plan for your music.

Contours

If you are singing a recitative and no one else is speaking with you, you must find the contours of your conversation. If you are singing with someone, or, often in opera, multiple people, you need to think practically.

- Who in the group speaks the fastest?
- Who in the group speaks the slowest?

For example, in *Le nozze di Figaro* by Mozart, who do you think speaks faster between Susanna and Bartolo? That's easy. It would be Susanna! But who speaks faster in the following pairs: the Countess or the Count, Cherubino or Susanna, Figaro or Marcellina? You will need to dig into the entire story to help you with this. But working with an experienced coach or linguist will absolutely get you into the right ballpark. Your own character will also sometimes speak more quickly and sometimes more slowly. Know the nuances of speed as it applies to your character.

Rhythm

People typically do not speak in exact rhythms, but composers are obligated to set specific rhythms for the pitches and text so that their vision can be sung in a specific way. This is where you, as a singer, must lift the words off the page and make them come to life as if they were your own. Where the composer stresses the word in the sentence is a clear indicator of where you need to go. It is my belief that rhythms don't change. Composers set them for a reason, and we need to respect that. However, the **tempo does change**. And with the fluidity of tempo and rubato (which comes from the Italian verb *to steal*) you will be able to find a shape that sounds natural.

Here's a fun, quick little exercise to clarify this point:

- Speak your own name in a sentence that goes something like this: "My name is Angela O'Brien."
- Now write the sentence in a rhythm. (In this case I would use a triplet for "My name is," four sixteenth notes for "Angela O," and two eighth notes for "Brien."
- Say it a few times.
- Now ask a singer friend to speak this in rhythm.
- You will always find that suddenly rhythm takes precedence, and the text takes a back seat. What started out as a genuine sentence from you, is written down to the best of your ability, shared with someone else, and is usually spoken in a stilted manner.

This is how it is with recitative!

Reaction words

Another part of normal conversation is the natural overlap of speaking. Everyone doesn't politely close their mouth and wait a beat and then speak. Why do singers do this in recitative? I think it is because the words go by so quickly and it takes a moment to register that the line before their line is finished. You do not want big gaping holes in the recitative unless a stage director has brilliantly filled it for you. So, what do you do?

You find "reaction words." These are words that have some significance for your character that would stimulate a normal response. I encourage you to circle them or highlight them. For example, in Mozart's *Così fan tutte,* Fiordiligi and Dorabella sing a recitative prior to the famous duet "Prenderò quel brunettino."

Fiordiligi: *Sorella, cosa dici?* (Sister, what do you say?)
Dorabella: *Io son stordita dallo spirto infernal di tal ragazza.* (I am dumbfounded by the hellish spirit of that girl)

Fiordiligi: *Ma crediti: è una pazza. Ti par che siam in caso di seguir suoi consigli?* (But believe you me, she is crazy. Does it seem to you, in this case, that we should follow her advice?)

If you wait for the full sentence to end before you breathe and sing, the recitative becomes stilted, choppy, and seemingly endless. So, choose your words. I've indicated ideas in **bold**. When you hear that word, you have a reaction that precipitates your entrance. You also need to know the last word, so you know when to come in (it is in **bold** as well).

Fiordiligi: *Sorella, **cosa dici**?* (Sister, what do you say?)
Dorabella: *Io son stordita dallo **spirto** infernal di tal **ragazza**.* (I am dumbfounded by the hellish spirit of that girl)
Fiordiligi: *Ma crediti: è una **pazza**. Ti par che siam in caso di seguir suoi **consigli**?* (But believe you me, she is crazy. Does it seem to you, in this case, that we should follow her advice?)

The word choices are totally yours. But if you focus on your words, it is perfect for the beginning linguist to remember only two words rather than the entire sentence in the beginning of the learning process.

Fiordiligi: *Sorella, **cosa dici**?* (Dorabella is always ready to have an opportunity to speak, so the whole line creates a thought. It is also a very short sentence.)
Dorabella: ***spirto** .... **Ragazza*** (Fiordiligi hears SPIRITED and GIRL. Reaction on spirited. Prepares her *Ma* then is ready to sing right after the word girl)
Fiordiligi: *Ma crediti: è una **pazza**. Ti par che siam in caso di seguir suoi **consigli**?* (Dorabella reacts to *pazza*/CRAZY and jumps in after the word ADVICE.)

For the novice ear it could sound like this:
*Lalala **cosa dici***
*Lalalalala**spirto**lalalalala**ragazza***
*Lalalalalala**pazza**lalalalalalalala**consigli***

It gets you in the ballpark and helps your reaction appear to be the result of understanding what is being said and answering in an authentic manner.

Appoggiatura

To appoggiatura or not to appoggiatura? Technically an appoggiatura is an ornament, an added pitch that is not in the chord and falls on the downbeat, resolving to a pitch in the chord. Appoggiatura comes from the Italian verb *appoggiare*, which means to lean (a word we also use to describe breath support as appoggio). What are we leaning into? We are leaning on a dissonant pitch with a resolution to a tone in the chord. There are many opinions and many different styles of music to consider. For many composers, appoggiaturas were not written out. It was presumed that the singer had the skillsets necessary to execute them and the musical understanding of where to put them. Bach, on the other hand, usually wrote out his appoggiaturas. In recitative, appoggiaturas help the line sound more melodic and can help show many different emotional facets. Expression is the main and best (for me) justification for or against appoggiaturas; they are very personal. Listen to multiple recordings of one recitative and notate where the appoggiaturas are. Use different colored pencils for each singer and mark the appoggiatura with an X above it. It's interesting to see who chooses what. A good book to consult for this and many other performance and stylistic matters is noted in the appendix. Elliott, Martha. *Singing in Style: A Guide to Vocal Performance Practices.* New Haven, Connecticut, Yale University Press, 2008.

Process for learning a recitative (not for the faint of heart)

I have a specific process that I suggest for singers. Hold on!

- Read the recitative in the original language.
- Translate it to English (using the translation template).
- Read the recitative in English.
- If story comes from an original source, read the original source.
- If the story is historical—do a bit of research to contextualize what you are saying.
- Work the recitative as dialogue.
  - What do you have to say?
  - What are you hearing?
  - Why are you in conversation?
  - Find places to interact.
- Choose one word to start with for reaction to what is being said to you in the conversation.
- Practicing your recitative—"Slow and steady wins the race."
- Write your text on 3x5 cards.
  - Speak the text on the cards.
- Start speaking with two to three syllables to gain fluency, then shift to three to four syllables, etc.
- Once you have reached fluency with that sentence, sing the sentence on one pitch—following the contour of the sentence.
- Once you have reached fluency with the full recitative, read the words with feeling while your pianist/coach lightly plays the harmonies on the keyboard.
- On subsequent readings, the pianist/coach can lightly play the singer's pitches in time to the spoken text.
  - This is helpful, as the vocal line will become entwined with the text before you even begin to sing.
- As you do all of this, concurrently:
  - Learn the rhythm of your recitative and speak it on "da" or "la," or tap it out.
  - Once the rhythm is mastered, learn the pitches, again on "da" or "la," or a syllable of your choice.
- Merge your learning—singing the correct text, pitches, and rhythms—one line at a time, or one chunk at a time.
- Vary the speeds, but never forsake accuracy and correctness of text authenticity or correct pitches/rhythms.
- Additional practice methods to employ:
  - Speak the text slowly.
  - Speak the text very fast (warp speed).
  - Speak the text in rhythm with a metronome set to a slow speed. Choose a setting that allows for 100% accuracy, usually this is around ♩ = 60 on the metronome, but feel free to start slower. Each time you achieve 100% accuracy, increase the speed on the metronome by two (from 60 to 62) until you are speaking it in rhythm much faster than you will ever have to sing it.

When you get above 145 or so, you might need to increase the speed only by one.

- Mark (sing lightly) in English, lining up the English words for an exact match where the Italian words are. You might need to add notes or change rhythms to accomplish this, but this helps solidify your understanding of what exactly you are saying.

For example, in Dorabella's aria from Mozart's *Così fan tutte,* the English words would replace, AT THE SAME POINT, the Italian words

Chiudi	*quelle*	*finestre …*	*Odio*	*la*	*luce…*
You close	that	window…	I hate	the	light

Figure 46: Mozart, *Così fan tutte*, "Ah scostati" recit before "Smanie implacabili"

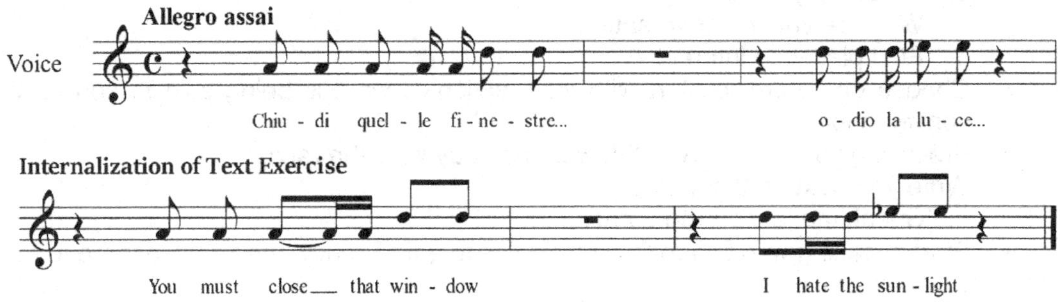

Part 1.8

Improving Your Sight Singing Skills

When I was a child, nothing made me happier on a rainy weekend than to pull out my mom's difficult piano music and sight read for hours. Subsequently, I became unafraid to sight read, and became quite proficient at it.

But how often is a singer asked to sight read? If the singer is in a choral ensemble, the answer is: On a regular basis. Sight singing skills are critical in that arena. And most young opera or classical singers make a significant portion of their income singing in church choirs, opera choruses, and other community ensembles. Many professional singers find great joy (as well as a lucrative income) singing in the opera choruses of the largest opera houses in the world. Many young artist programs enlist their participants to sing in their chorus. Even if you are not part of a choral ensemble, strong sight singing skills can help the learning process in all your repertoire.

Every choral audition that I've attended required a sight singing portion. I'm not sure statistically how many singers get the sight singing 100% right, but when they do it is positively noted. These singers will have a much better handle on the demands of singing with a new music ensemble where sight singing difficult repertoire is expected.

There are multiple resources available on sight reading/sight singing. If you simply google "sight reading for singing," multiple options are listed. Colleges and universities offer mandatory sight-singing courses for music majors and many also offer introductory courses for non-majors. Please thoroughly invest yourselves in these classes; too many singers fail to understand the importance of musical literacy. By the time they graduate, most instrumentalists can sight-read at tempo and will have played a significant portion of the important repertoire written for their instrument. Too many singers, however, finish their degrees with a package of five arias, which they learned by rote with little depth to their work.

No matter your skill level in this crucial activity, you can find your entry point. It is vital that you diligently work to become musically literate so that you can approach your music with specific skills and knowledge. Imagine how efficient you will be when learning new repertoire, trying out a variety of repertoire, sight singing successfully at church jobs and chorus rehearsals; your speed of learning will increase, which will help your confidence soar. I cannot stress enough how important this is. Hire a tutor. Practice sight singing daily. Develop a system.

The three required skills include pitches, rhythms, and words. In many sight singing auditions, there are no words. The singer can sing on a syllable of their choice or choose solfège. If you choose solfège, you will need to decide whether to use fixed *do* or movable *do*. If these terms are foreign to you, I suggest you revisit your notes from freshman music theory or take an online course to become proficient in sight singing or buy a book that guides you in your study. Like so many things, sight reading/sight singing is here to stay. The good news is that you can get better!

Practice steps for sight singing

- Look at the time signature, key signature, and tempo indication. Make sure you are clear whether the excerpt is in major or minor.
- Take a closer look for additional markings such as accidentals, meter changes, or tempo changes.
- Establish a clear tempo.
- Give yourself the starting pitch, or the tonic triad.
- Review the rhythmic pattern in your head
- Identify the half steps, whole steps, and the skips to know exactly what they are
- Look for any repeating patterns
- Sing any difficult skips or passages in your head
- Sing through the entire excerpt in your head
- Sight sing the excerpt, recording your attempt
- Use a keyboard to see how accurate you were
- Play back the recording to check for accuracy as well

Sight singing skills should be practiced daily. Don't despair, however, it only takes five minutes a day to ensure you habituate sight singing into your routine. The more you do it, the better you will become. Once a week give yourself the challenge of looking at the piece for only 20 seconds and see how much you can sing correctly in a timed situation.

Resources you might have access to for free

If you are part of a church choir, or just a member of a church, ask the Music Director if you can borrow a hymnal to take home to practice your sight singing (or check one out from your library). This is a good place to start, and no matter your voice type, it is good practice to sing each of the four voice parts in your vocal range so that you widen your ability and strengthen your ear and sight singing skills—not to mention providing sopranos with an opportunity to read lines that are not the melody. If you are a student, see what additional resources are in your library and check them out.

Some online resources are likely to be free.

Look at your own music collection. If everything you have includes text, eliminate the text in the beginning. When you start to integrate the text, you will need to add the following steps:

- Identify the language of the piece.
- Speak the text in your head, looking for any pronunciation stumbling blocks that you might encounter (for example two vowels on one note in Italian, the ç-laut or x-laut in German, liaisons or schwas in French).
- Speak the text in rhythm in your head.

Have courage! The more successful you become with sight singing, the easier your music learning will become.

Part 1.9

Working in Cooperation with Voice Teachers

Voice Teachers

Singers have a team of people to help them achieve their goals. It is so important that we work together. The singer/teacher relationship is very close; so is the singer/coach relationship.

I am always happy to chat with voice teachers about their students, their progress, and their challenges; the more we can communicate, the more effective we can be. I check in regularly with the students I coach with phrases such as, "what would your teacher think about how you sang that phrase?" or "what would your teacher suggest you do to sing this phrase in tune?" It is a voice teacher's job is to teach technique, not a coach. But as a vocal coach, I'll happily work on all the elements that aren't technique. It can be very confusing to singers, especially young singers, when the coach crosses the line and starts talking about vocal technique.

When singers transition from undergraduate school to graduate school, I ask them what they need in their next teacher (graduate school choice, in my opinion, should be about the teacher first). Who will give you what you need next? You need to know this. If I were going to host an outdoor barbeque for twenty people, I would not prepare for the party by going to buy groceries at a jewelry store. As a singer, you need to know what skills you need to acquire. A conversation with your current teacher as you contemplate graduate schools is a good step in the right direction. Processing all of this with your coach, and other team members, is also a wise choice. Honesty from your team and you is the only way to grow and make solid, good choices.

Do you hear what I hear?

I am always truthful about what I hear; I would lose credibility if it were otherwise. I usually tell the singer several things they have done well, and then I tell them what they need to work on and why. I also give them practice tools. I may think I know the technical reason for what I'm hearing, but I will never suggest it with technical terms. My offerings include, "When you get to the top of the staff in this piece, your sound loses focus, and you seem to be singing on the high side of the pitch." "Look in the mirror when you sing this time and let me know if what you are doing is what your teacher would like for you to do." "Sing this as if it were an octave higher, without really singing it an octave higher."

I always ask for singer feedback, "How did that feel?" "Would your teacher approve?" Sometimes we may need to try several things before we get to the "ah-ha!" I will also frequently ask the student to share what we discovered in our coaching with their teacher in their next lesson.

Repertoire

It is such a pleasure helping guide singers to repertoire or roles that are suitable for them. It is a bit tricky, however, with younger voices, who, in a decade might sing much heavier repertoire, but for the time need to work on music that is less demanding vocally. Again, the marriage between the teacher and coach can be crucial during these discussions and decisions.

If you sing for someone once and they tell you that you are singing all the wrong repertoire and make suggestions for something radically different, it is okay to ask them why they are suggesting this (in a polite manner). But then, take it back to your team to vet the reality. When I have given feedback after auditions, I rarely would call for an entire repertoire overhaul, even when I felt this would be the best thing. I would hear these hopeful singers for all of ten minutes. I would suggest that the pieces seemed to be too big a stretch for them. Was this a particularly tough day? Or is this the way it usually goes? I found the singers to be incredibly honest. I would preface that, "In my opinion, some alternative repertoire would serve you well because [explain why]. Perhaps you can have a conversation with your teacher and coach about this." One expert says a starter audition piece should be short and sweet. Another expert says the starter should put it all out on the line. Which is right? Who's to know?!?!?!

Singers and respect

I love and respect singers. They not only have to build a technique (like all musicians) but they have to build their instrument as well. A pianist or violinist often starts learning their instrument at three or four years of age, which is not as common, but certainly possible for singers. A budding vocalist can sing in choirs, begin their musicianship training and sight singing skills at a very early age. Every musician, except singers, purchases their instrument. The building of an instrument takes time, care, love, consideration, health, and so many more things. The best thing coaches and teachers can do is to work cooperatively to their benefit. I'm in. Are you?

Part 2: Daily Non-Musical Tools

When you're too tired to sing

When I suggest to singers that they spend four to six hours a day practicing, I am fully aware that it is impossible to sing full steam ahead for that amount of time. A good practice day will include warming up, working on details vocally, practicing the performance of a piece, and all the non-singing activities necessary for comprehensive learning. Part 2 contains suggested activities to support the non-singing portion of daily practice.

Part 2.1

Working with Language

It is difficult enough to express yourself in your native language, so how in the world can we be expressive in a language that we don't truly speak? How can we convince the audience members that we are Italian as we nuance the recitatives in *Le nozze di Figaro,* or French as we sing the glorious vocal lines in *Werther,* or German in the dialogues of *Die Fledermaus?* There are relatively few true polyglots in our field, so what are we to do? We pretend, with confidence, as we gain our skills. And we work hard. We need so many tools at our disposal so that we can approach language from a multitude of directions. And, by the end of our careers, we usually are comfortable in multiple languages. But that doesn't help you when you are 22 years old.

Where language lives in your mouth

When speaking different languages, there is a natural gravitation to where the language wants to live. Speak the following phrases out loud several times and pay attention to where you feel the language.

- *Gute nacht*: do you feel the /x/ ach-laut?
- Good night: where do you feel your tongue on the roof of your mouth?
- *Buona notte*: where do you feel that true Italian double t?
- *Bonne nuit*: where do you feel the vowel glide /bɔn nɥi/

These places in your mouth give you a clue to the differences in where the languages lie. I don't want to get too close to "teacher territory," but I do know that if you speak your French text from your American place, you will never sound French.

Translating

As a singer, you need access to excellent dictionaries. It is not okay to have only one option for each word that you translate; you need to explore, around and behind the word to know what you truly mean. There is a three-tiered translation in the appendix that I have used in classes and with private students for a very long time. This allows you the opportunity to look at the text in the original language, in a word for word translation (offering multiple translations for each word), a transliteration (shifting the text from one language to another language), and a contemporary translation in your own words. The first three lines need not change over time, so once you do the work well, you are set for life! Only your personal way to say the transliteration will shift after life experience, time, reading, etc. Moral: do it well the first time so that you truly understand what you're saying.

1.

Sebben,	*crudele,*	*mi*	*fai*	*languir (languire)*

2.

Though	cruel	me	you make	languish
Although	harsh		you do	pine away
	savage		you have	grow faint
	unkind		you are	weaken
	merciless		you act	
	heartless		you get	
	pitiless			
	hard-hearted			

3.
Though, cruel one, me you make languish

4.
Although, cruel one, you make me languish

Remember that the words *ma, mais,* and *aber* mean *but*, and that the word *but* usually changes the direction of the sentence. This will always be an important word when translating and choosing color for your sound.

Speaking

In this section, you will find practice tools for working the text into your mouth. The tool is the same for all languages, but I'll use an Italian example here, "Sebben, crudele, mi fai languir."

- Choose two syllables in the middle of the sentence, *dele*. Speak the two syllables out loud and in different tempi multiple times. Be sure that you use a single Italian /l/.
- When it feels comfortable and natural, add in a third syllable, and do the same, *dele mi*.
- Drop the first syllable, add the syllable after *mi*, *le mi fa*, and do the same.
- Drop the first syllable, add the syllable after *fa*, *mi fai*, and do the same.
- Drop the *fai* and add *cru* to the *dele mi*, *crudele* with multiple repetitions.
- Continue dropping the first or last of the three syllables and add a syllable to the right or the left of the group and practice speaking them out loud in varying tempi.
- Do this until you have completed the entire sentence in three-syllable chunks.
- Next, find groups of four syllables and do the same.
- Finally, find groups of five syllables and do the same.

Remember that the composer was presented with words that were not set to rhythm. Once you know and understand how to speak the words, you'll understand more of the composer's intent in the rhythmic and pitch setting.

After completing the steps above, you may continue as follows:

- Sing the sentence on one pitch with the rhythm driven by the text. Keep the language fluent but have a slightly different tempo on each repetition.
- Now sing the sentence on one pitch in the rhythm indicated by the composer.

But how do you transfer the language facility to true understanding? I ask my singers to mark (sing lightly) the vocal line, in English, as if they were in a hotel room at 3:00 am, were desperate to practice, but didn't want to get kicked out of the hotel. Or I'll request, "sing in a tiny, small, coachy voice." (If you don't know how to mark, please ask your teacher immediately!) The English needs to be word for word, just like the translation, which might mean adding or taking away some notes to align exactly with the original (see example in Part 1.8.). This helps your brain understand what the English words are in the same place as the foreign language. If you are a native speaker, you will more easily retain and understand the meaning and text.

Other exercises include speaking the text in rhythm with the metronome, from very slow (♩ = 40 to 60, to ♩ = 180 to 204). Move the metronome up only two notches at a time. This begins as a slow and steady reinforcement of all the skills learned. You will notice that you will likely go from the trot to the gallop. In horseback riding, the trot is faster than the walk, but the ride is usually a bit bumpy. In the gallop, all four feet are off the ground at the same time in a long stride. In speaking your text, this happens when you are truly legato and don't let the consonants bump you around or off! Once you've achieved a full gallop and can go faster than you'll ever need, the words will form easily in your mouth and singing will be much easier.

Once you are comfortable with full sentences, spoken at a native speed, you can pair that with the flashcards from Part 1!

- Write out all your texts on 3x5 cards, one sentence at a time.
- Practice one card at a time, multiple times gaining fluency and a native flair.
- Choose a text card and choose an attitude card. Don't stop to think about how to do it, just speak it with that attitude

And finally, recite your text as poetry or a story. Record your recitation and listen back. Does it sound authentic? Do you have something to say in your interpretation of the story or poem?

Other ideas for language learning

Now that we have some of the basics down, there are so many fun activities to help us grow linguistically or keep our languages fresh.

- There are many free cartoons, movies, television programs and readings on YouTube and other online platforms. Some are subtitled, some are not.
- There are many free games to play in the various languages online for all levels.
- Visit a public library and check out a children's book in a foreign language. Most public libraries sell some of their books from time to time. See what they have to offer in the children's section in foreign languages. You'll only pay a small amount of money to

have a book you can read. Read it to yourself, read it out loud, read it to friends in your singing circle to see if they can follow the story.

- Seek out books, magazines, poetry, and crossword puzzles in foreign languages at libraries, bookstores, online, or when you travel out of the country. There are even books that have the story in the foreign language on the left page with the English on the right page.
- During school, take language classes, even if they are not required. In my opinion, two years each of Italian, German, and French are the basics. You'll never regret language classes.
- In the summer take classes at local community colleges, online, or in private study.
- Find a conversation partner or conversation table at your university or community for whichever language you are studying. If one doesn't exist, create one.
- After graduation from university classes, continue working on your languages. Choose one language per year to focus on and rotate each year.
- Take a language course in the country where it is spoken. Be sure, if you do this, that after class time is over, you don't speak English with your friends for the rest of the day. Venture out and practice speaking with the native speakers. In my experience, they are grateful that you are taking the time to learn their language.

Pesky language issues

I'm sure that there is a longer list than I will present here, but the following represents some of the peskiest issues that come up regularly with singers. There are also many language resources online as well as textbooks that can help with the basics and specifics of languages.

- Diphthongs. In most instances, the first vowel of the diphthong is the dominant vowel. This is especially obvious if you shift to the second vowel too early when holding a long note.
- Phrases that keep tripping you up. What do you do? Build bridges! You break the problem down to the smallest common denominator (two vowels) and practice slowly. You bridge the words together two syllables at a time.
    - An example is in "Deh vieni, non tardar," from *Le nozze di Figaro.* Susanna has the very difficult cluster of vowels in the phrase *finché l'aria è ancor*, I am forever hearing the phrase with one or more of them missing. Go back to the two syllables (in this case the tricky syllables are unique vowels) exercise, then three vowels, and continue in the pattern detailed above.
- Italian issues
    - Double consonants (no explosions or pops, please)
    - The Italian letter T (no explosions or pops here either, please)
    - Final syllables (last syllable-itus). Remember that unless the last syllable is accented the stress is on the penultimate syllable. To practice this, say *Mamma mia*. We usually say that correctly. Or use your own name if the stress is on the next to the last syllable, such as Michael, Carol, Latonya, Gracie.
    - There are only seven vowel sounds, so keep them as pure as possible.
    - The Italian letter U; in *quando, questo, Gualtiero.* While it is written in the IPA as a /w/, the Italian alphabet does not include the letter /w/. Go through the /u/ quickly to get to the next vowel and you will find that your mouth shape and space is less wide and better for a focused sound

  - Practice the language with a pencil or your finger in your mouth (between your teeth). You'll see how little your jaw and tongue must move for clear language.
  - Some Italian singers I love to listen to for their beautiful use of their own language include Luciano Pavarotti, Mirella Freni, Beniamino Gigli, Enrico Caruso, Ettore Bastianini, Renata Scotto, Giuseppe Di Stefano, Franco Corelli, Renata Tebaldi, Ezio Pinza, Tito Gobbi, Carlo Bergonzi, Cesare Siepi, Italo Tajo, Nicola Rossi-Lemeni, Piero Cappuccilli, Giulietta Simionata, Paolo Montarsolo.
- French issues
  - The schwa. Native French speakers do not look at the IPA of a schwa and pronounce it like we do in American English. The closest approximation of the French schwa is /oe/. Experiment with how open your mouth can be and still have the integrity of the French schwa.
  - /m/ and /n/ in the middle of words or ends of words that only serve to nasalize vowels. We know the rules, but we do it anyway: we pronounce them in the middle or ends of words, such as *fond du* or *dangereuse*. We do this, I believe, by accident. Our own language has us frequently moving through the /m/ and /n/s as we close our mouths. To avoid this, say each syllable with a large space in between. Get used to the sound and the feel. Then start to shorten the space in between. Eventually, you will get to a legato and fluid pronunciation without being interrupted by those pesky consonants.
  - The U, transliterated in IPA as /y/. must be attended to for the vowel correctly to sound French. Begin with the /i/ sound. Now pucker your lips. The only thing that should change is your lips. The vowel of /i/ stays consistent.
  - Silent endings in speaking versus singing. This is just a caution to remind you that the endings in singing can vary from speaking. The biggest example is the silent schwa. For example, if you are speaking the word *parle*, there is no schwa; however, if you are singing it, and there is a note, you are obligated to sing the /oe/ sound. *Faites attention* (pay attention) to this difference.
  - Liaison. When to use a liaison (pronouncing a consonant that normally is silent) is the eternal question. When I started out the rules were pretty much hard and fast; now they have become more flexible. The biggest rule to remember is that if the liaison changes the meaning of the text, you should not do it.
  - Some French singers I love to listen to for their beautiful use of their own language include Régine Crespin, Michel Sénéchal, Gerard Souzay, Martial Singher, Natalie Dessay, Roberto Alagna, Lily Pons, Mireille Delunsch, Sabine Devieilhe, Annick Massis, Germaine Lubin, Gerard Serkoyan, Thierry Gregoire, and Edith Piaf.
- German issues
  - The *ich-laut*, found after the vowels I and E, is a difficult sound for many native English speakers. Too often we mispronounce this as the /ʃ/ in the word 'should.' The closest approximation can be found in the following English sentence in how we pronounce the /h/:. *Huge humans of every hue live in Houston.*
  - The *ach-laut* is the guttural, throaty ch that is found after the vowels A, O, and U. It is often described as a voiceless velar fricative. If you exhale with the focus on the back part of the roof of your mouth you are likely able to feel and hear a slightly guttural sound. Unfortunately, there are no English words to help with the ach-laut.
  - The umlaut is a lovely and strange concept. I find it fascinating that it started out as either an E after—or even above—the A, O, or U, but in a smaller font. It is now usually represented by two dots above the vowel (ä, ö, ü, Ä, Ö, Ü). You may also write them (generally) as ae, oe, or ue.
    - The Ä is pronounced as an open or closed e depending on the word

        - The Ö also has the open or closed e in the mouth, but with slightly puckered, rounded lips. To practice this, say /e/ or /ɛ/ and slowly shift to the puckered position. Once you get used to the feel, it will be easy.
    - The Ü can be open or closed and has /I/ or /i/ as the vowel inside your mouth and /u/ as the vowel at your lips. To practice the open version, as in the word *Küss* (kiss), speak or sing the /I/ sound while closing your lips to an /u/ shape, which results in the phonetic /Y/. To create the closed form, as in the word *Frühling* (spring), speak or sing the /i/ sound, again closing your lips to the /u/. You now are making the correct sound for /y/.
    - The schwa is like Coke and Pepsi. People usually have a strong preference. You can find books and documentation for the accuracy of most preferences. However, I usually default to what many German singers told me when I was working there. I was told that they simply keep the basic mouth position of the preceding vowel and let the schwa fall in that position, which makes sense to me.
    - Legato. You often hear singers say that "German has so many consonants it is not possible to sing legato." This is a false statement. Listen to the singers on the list below and each one will defy this thought, especially Wunderlich. Legato is essential in all music making. Don't make an exception in the German language.
    - PF as in *Pferd* (horse). "Hip flask." And I must give credit where credit is due. I learned this combination during the time I played for weekly classes in the home of a true polyglot, Nico Castel.
    - Some German singers I love to listen to for their beautiful use of their own language include Fritz Wunderlich, Elizabeth Schwartzkopf, Hans Hotter, Herman Prey, Dietrich Fisher-Dieskau, Christa Ludwig, Kurt Moll, Hildegard Behrens, Jonas Kaufmann, Brigitte Fassbaender, Diana Damrau, Réne Pape

English issues

Be sure to translate your English. Unless it is truly colloquial and you understand every nuance, there are usually many words that you will need to translate. Good examples of this include works by Roger Quilter, Benjamin Britten, and Igor Stravinsky. Using the IPA in your English repertoire also can help you avoid regionalisms that occur in your vernacular speech.

Part 2.2

Marking Your Music

A new score is exciting to own. There is so much to explore and cultivate from the printed page. A score with your markings, however, is priceless. It is a road map for your learning.

So, what exactly gets marked on the page and how is it marked? This might seem simple, but I have worked with so many singers who forget to mark things in their score. They think: "This is so important, I'll remember it—no need to write it down," and then, months later, the singer is paying for the same information a second time. In addition to your own well-marked score, you need one for your pianist. And the two versions are very different from each other.

To prepare for marking your music, you will need at least one highlighter and a set of colored pencils, or the digital equivalent if you are using a tablet or computer to read your score. Then, you need a system. Here are some suggestions for marking your personal score, but if you find a way that works for you, please use that system. Specific tools for specific markings, however, are suggested.

- Highlight all tempo indicators and changes. This way, when you see the bright yellow (or whatever color you choose) you will know before you get there that a tempo change is coming up.
- Circle dynamics in red pencil. This way, when you see the red, you know a dynamic change is coming up. For *sotto voce* mark a large, bold, red SV before it begins if it is preceded by a rest, or on it, if it occurs suddenly. The composer had a specific timbre in mind when writing *sotto voce*; it is up to us to respect and implement that choice.
- For articulations choose a different color pencil. This way staccato, *detachée*, or portamenti won't be overlooked. When thinking about articulation, I encourage singers to place their right-hand fingers on their lower left arm; tapping up and down (where the fingers leave the arm) is like staccato, giving yourself a "mini-massage" is like legato, and pulsing on your arm (without your fingers leaving your arm) is like *detachée*. These are physical feelings that can complement the understanding of musical articulations.
- Breath marks should be big and bold once you've determined where you need to breathe. A regular pencil is recommended, as your choice might change over time.
- If a particular metronome marking is helpful for you, mark it in your score. If a pianist asks you for your preferred tempo, a metronome number is much more accurate than if you attempt to mark or sing the tempo (especially quickly at the piano before an audition). I find that most of the tempi sung in that manner are not what the singer truly wants. When I would play auditions, I would simply say, "If my tempo is too fast or too slow, change it when you come in. I will follow you." But a metronome marking will get everyone in the same ballpark.
- If you find it helpful to use descriptive words for verses or phrases, the small sticky notes can be helpful. This allows for change as you change and grow as a musician, and as your understanding of the piece deepens.
- Where do you put your translation? I suggest, in your practice copy, to translate above the text so that each time you say a word, for example *Una furtiva lagrima,* would have "a secret tear" (or however you chose to translate *furtiva*) above it and the IPA

underneath it. If you are more advanced with language, you will need less IPA and fewer words translated. But you always need to know exactly what the word is when you are singing it. You need to make sure the meaning is practiced with everything else.

- Put in your cuts clearly. This can be done with sticky notes and/or bold lines. Traditionally, cuts in the score are indicated with the word *vide* in brackets. The beginning of the cut is marked [vi- and its end is labeled -de]. Sometimes a line from the VI to the DE is visually helpful. So, what does the VI-DE represent? That the music in between is omitted or cut. (When you receive a "cut list" from an upcoming job, you immediately need to put those cuts in your score. I encourage learning the entire role but knowing the cuts when you arrive at rehearsal is imperative. And, sometimes a cut is "opened" once rehearsals have started, so learning the whole score is necessary. The word *vide* has many origins. I am not an etymologist, nor will I offer the definitive answer to the meaning, but there are three various thoughts. *Vide* in Latin is the imperative "to look," perhaps meaning to look for the end of the word for where you begin again. *Vide* in French means empty, so the measures between *Vi* and *de* are empty. And *vide* in Italian means "to see" and musically the implication as always meant "empty." The Italian word *vuota* also means empty, but that refers to a measure that is silent (no one plays or sings).

When you work with a pianist, you must provide them with a different copy of your music. They do not need to know all the details that you have put in, but they do need crucial information, and a discussion at the piano during an audition takes away from your singing time. A well-marked score is all you need.

- First, when you've copied your music, make sure that all the pitches, words, and indications are clean and clear. It is never okay to leave out the bass clef at the bottom, which, sadly, often happens. Similarly, make sure that the top, sides, and any instructions about the piece are clear and easy to read. This might sound basic—it is—but it also often is overlooked.
- Make sure you copy your music (songs, arias, and ensembles) back-to-back, and that the pagination is presented like it is in the original source. Never use staples if you don't have access to a double-sided copier as they can injure the pianist's fingers in a quick page turn. Securing each edge with tape, or even the old-fashioned way with rubber cement is better than staples, but back-to-back is the best. Unless your personal pianist specifically requests this, do not copy accordion style where the six- to seven-page aria or song doesn't really fit on the music rack of the piano.
- Turn each page and slightly crumple the lower right-hand corner of the page. Freshly copied music often does not turn well and can hinder the smooth audition or rehearsal that you envision.
- Put in the essential markings. You don't want to leave anything to chance.
    - Cuts (I once had a singer glibly state, "standard cuts." This does not work, because there are often several "standard cut" options.)
    - Breath marks (This lets the pianist know where you will breathe, enabling them to help accommodate that in their playing)
    - Highlight or circle in red anything that is important to your interpretation, including tempo shifts, fermatas, meter changes, and dynamics. This will help the sight-reading pianist. (I have had a few singers indicate that a pianist took offense at the markings, as the pianist felt it suggested a compromised musicianship. I consider

it a gift, as it is a roadmap for the way you want me to use to get to your destination.)
    - Include a metronome range or specific marking when possible (e.g. ♩ = 60). This will help the pianist understand your tempo as most pianists have used metronomes all their lives in one way or another.
    - Remember that the pianist can only be expected to do what the music is asking. They can read your gesture, breath, and sound, but not your mind. Don't leave anything to chance!
- Put your copied music in a medium or small size binder. Don't bring your biggest binder with your entire repertoire in it for a coaching or an audition. Be thoughtful and "right size" the binder.
    - Do not put your music in protective sleeves as the glare from the lights can render it unreadable.
    - Do tab your music by aria title, composer, or opera, however you introduce it. It needs to be consistent and alphabetical. Computer generated tabs are better than handwritten. It's tricky when the panelists ask for "the Mozart" if you don't have Mozart on a tab and the pianist is less experienced, or when they ask for Papageno and you've tabbed it as "Ein Mädchen oder Weibchen." Know how your system works so that if what is requested doesn't match your tab, you can simply turn to the pianist (do not walk to their side) and let them know which tab the selection is under.

Part 2.3

Telling the Story in Your Music

Music has told stories for generations. I remember dancing in full costume (well, actually just my mom's old prom slip) to Mussorgsky's *Night On Bald Mountain* as a five year old. The story spoke to me. And most of us are familiar with Prokofiev's famous tale, *Peter and the Wolf.* Instruments take on personalities with which we can identify through timbre and color. We hear the bird in the flute, the duck in the oboe, the cat in the clarinet, and of course the grandfather in the bassoon.

In vocal music, we are fortunate enough to have words that help tell the story. In opera, we add sets, costumes, make-up, wigs, and other people. But just how do we integrate that storytelling into our music making? It is key to be able to color and shape your sound without those external trappings.

If you see a friend in the distance and you want to connect, you don't usually have to ponder what expression to use: you raise your voice in a manner that is louder, friendly, and specific to get their attention. Likewise, when telling someone about your great news, you don't spend unnecessary time thinking about tone, inflection, and the like. You let your genuine enthusiasm shine though as you talk about your good news. This is how we communicate. You all can do it. You all have been doing it your entire life. Why stop when it comes to singing?

You already have years of experience being *you*. You know what your routines are, what you like, what you dislike, what you did last week, what you did last year. In vocal music, you need to create that for each character that you portray. You know how frustrating it is when someone else is telling your story and getting the facts wrong? (Thought bubble, "No the city was not New York but Chicago. No, the role was not Don Ottavio but you did get Mozart right.") The same is true for characters. If you do not pay attention to what the score indicates or include additional research, you could get some basic facts wrong about who you are portraying.

The thought of an in-depth analysis may make you quake with fear. But take a deep breath and realize that you are simply being a super sleuth investigating the character you are portraying. Entire books have been written on this subject and it is not my intent to replicate the brilliance of their authors here (see Appendix: *Acting and drama resources*). However, I must point out that this is essential homework for you to undertake.

Reading the libretto is key to understanding the story. Can you synthesize the plot of the opera into one sentence? What is your character's part in this story? Does the story take place in one day, like *Le nozze di Figaro,* or over an extended period, like *La traviata?* When you read the libretto, take notes like a detective. This is **Libretto Analysis**, which is the core to understanding just about everything to come.

Who am I? What do I need? How old am I? What do I think about everyone else that I see and with whom I speak? How do I usually express my thoughts and feelings? What have I been doing for the past year? The answers to these questions are part of the **Character**

Analysis. "To know thyself is the beginning of wisdom." (Socrates). Simply "To know thyself," is sufficient. So, you must know the details of the person you are pretending to be and trying to convince us you are.

You need to know the details of time, place, setting, lighting, environment, and more. This is the **Environment Analysis**. In the book *"Singing, Acting, and Movement in Opera,"* by Mark Ross Clark there are templates for a variety of analyses. Clark, Mark Ross. *Singing, Acting, and Movement in Opera.* Bloomington, Indiana, Indiana University Press, 2002.

If I were singing Musetta's "Quando me'n vo," I might write the following:

> I have just arrived at Café Momus after a shopping spree with my current "benefactor," Alcindoro. It is bustling with the energy and excitement of Christmas Eve. It is cold, but I'm wrapped in furs and expensive, warm clothing. I'm hungry and look forward to a glass of wine before going home to inspect all the wonderful gifts/purchases. Suddenly, I see my ex… Marcello. Everything changes.

This is the beginning of a **Scene Analysis.** Where am I? Where did I come from? Do I know anyone here? Who is with me?

Do you see how essential the dramatic underpinning is to the integration of text and singing?

I like to think of creative ways to achieve these goals. After you have done the preliminary work outlined above, here are some fun ways to put it into action.

- Journal as your character for a week.
- Perform a daily activity (cooking, getting dressed, driving your car) as your character.
- Walk for a block as one character. After crossing the street, walk as another character. Trust me, these days no one will look at you oddly.
- Write a letter as your character.
- Chat with a friend as your character. See if they can guess who you are!
- Imagine your character two years from the final measure of your aria. What has happened? Allow your choices in this creative exercise to be informed by the context and given circumstances of the opera—not necessarily the literal happenings in the story already created by the composer and librettist.
- Create your own costume from online research. How would it feel to wear that style of clothing? How might it inform who you are and how you move?

So, what about art songs? How do you bring the same depth to the drama? Often you get to make up the back-story. Other times, it is part of a whole. If you sing Schumann's *Frauenliebe und -Leben* you must read the entire original collection of poems. Read about the poet. Become the expert in your interpretation. If you sing "Claire de lune," by Fauré, you begin with the text and the translation (as mentioned earlier in the book) of the poem by Paul Verlaine. It helps then to read a bit about Verlaine to understand the perspective from which he writes. Next, you read a bit about the composer, you listen to the music, you look at the score, you use your imagination and creativity to envision what the composer was trying to achieve in how the text is set. What does the accompaniment portray, is it color or is it part of the story? To begin to start telling your story of the song, clearly mark where each verse is with numbers. Then choose three words to describe each verse. For example, in Schubert's "Die Forelle," the words for the first verse might be lively, spirited, and happy. The words are your choice, based on how you interpret the poem. Sometimes it is good to give each verse a color. For me, in the example above, I would use green as my color as a brook is found in nature. These tools immediately help define color and intent. Practicing the text alone with these prompts as well as the melody on your comfort vowel, help create the mood of the song from the beginning.

Part 2.4

The Research Behind What You Do

When I say research, you are probably going to break out in a sweat and panic or roll your eyes, but please don't. This is amazingly fun, and will help you understand what you are singing about in a deep and compelling way.

Read

Libretto. It is so important to know what the story is about. So, the first thing you need to do is read the entire libretto. Don't worry, you can read it in English! But I would find three or four translations of the libretto so that you get a full and comprehensive understanding of the story you are undertaking.

Original source material. If the opera or song is from an original source, the next step is to read the original source material. For example, if you are singing "Non so più," from *Le nozze di Figaro,* you will need to read the trilogy by Pierre-Augustin de Beaumarchais. The plays (in order and in French) are entitled *Le Barbier de Séville Ou la Précaution inutile, La Folle Journée ou Le Mariage de Figaro,* and *La Mère Coupable Ou L'Autre Tartuffe.* You likely know the first two from their Italian names, *Il barbiere di Siviglia* and *Le nozze di Figaro.* In English, the three titles are *The Barber of Seville, The Marriage of Figaro,* and *The Guilty Mother.* Your first step is to read *The Marriage of Figaro.* But do you stop there? No! You read the first play and discover that you are not in it! So, you read the third play and discover you are also not in it. BUT, you discover that you died in battle and that the Countess had your child. THIS informs how you play all of your part in *The Marriage of Figaro,* and most especially the steamy scene in Act 2 when you are momentarily alone with the Countess in her bedroom.

If you are singing a song cycle, read the original poetry so that you know if all the songs were set, and if not, ask yourself why. Read other poetry from the poet so you get a sense of the poet's artistic voice. Read out loud in English as well as the original language.

Other things to read. It also is fun to read the biographies of the composers and librettists as well as any books or collections of their letters and other writings. Find out whether the poem is usually taken literally or symbolically. You need to know, and constantly question, how to interpret the words. But the first steps are the libretto and original source.

All this reading will prompt you to ask questions:

- What was it like to live during that time?
- What did they wear and how did they style their hair or wig?
- Did they stand or walk in any special manner?
- What historical events should I be aware of during that time?

Let these questions lead to others. This is all kept in your notebook, as this research will last you your entire career. You want to keep track of it!

Look

After all your reading, or concurrently with the reading, start looking at pictures. Here is a list of things you might choose from. Again, let each picture take you to the next question and the next picture.

- Pictures from the time of the composer and librettist
- Pictures from the time of the opera
- Artwork from the time of the composer and librettist
- Artwork from the period of the opera
- Costumes from the period of the composer, librettist, and opera
- Daily dress from the time of the composer, librettist, and opera
- Formal dress from the time of the composer, librettist, and opera
- Hair and wig styles from the period of the composer, librettist, and opera
- Architecture from the time of the composer, librettist, and opera
- Pictures of any cities or regions represented in the opera from the period of the composer, librettist, or opera
- Pictures of the opera houses, both current and from the time of the composer, librettist, and opera

Many museums have opened their doors digitally so that more people can benefit and enjoy the art inside. Please take advantage of this opportunity unless you are fully funded and can travel the world going from museum to museum

Listen

No matter your preferred choice for sourcing recordings, there are so many at your disposal. No longer do you have to go to the library, sit at a listening room, then called a listening carrel, and spend your weekend deep in listening. You can listen from anywhere in the world! You can even watch arias, scenes, in fact, entire productions. Let YouTube and Google be your friends for learning. It is crucial to watch the aria you are singing as well as the entire opera. For songs, it is amazing how many different recordings you can access, so the same thing applies to all the song literature. When listening, keep track of cast lists. Get to know the names of the singers who sing your repertoire. Also, and this is so important, move away from listening only to living artists. There are so many amazing recordings available going back, even, 100 years. Listen to recordings from the 1930's. Listen to Toscanini conduct *La bohème* in the 1940's for RCA. There are even recordings you can find of Toscanini rehearsing and singing parts himself. This is valuable. This is gold.

With your specific repertoire, I suggest that you listen to ten recordings of the aria or song and keep track of what you hear. How do you do that? Start with a clean copy of your piece. Buy colored pencils that have, at least, ten colors in the package.

- Choose ten (or more) singers to listen to.
- Choose a color of pencil and on a sheet of paper preceding your music, write down the name of the singer, conductor, orchestra, and year.
- You might need to listen to each singer more than once. But you are going to capture, with that colored pencil, the following information.
  - Tempo (specific metronome marking if you can capture that)
  - Breath marks
  - Portamenti
  - Rallentandi
  - Cadenzas
  - Ornaments
  - All the little details that make that recording unique
- When finished with that singer's recording, move to the next, choose a different color of pencil and begin your listening again
- When you are finished with all ten, you will be an expert on that aria or song. You will know many artistic choices and options.

Note that you can choose a singer or conductor twice, provided the dates of the recordings are not near each other. This way you can also see the development of the musical style of the singer or conductor.

Other listening ideas include listening to non-opera or song repertoire by the composer. What makes that composer unique? Can you identify unifying factors between an orchestra piece, a string quartet, and an opera aria, for example?

I also often ask singers to move or dance to the music they are learning. What do their bodies want to do? What is the music asking of them physically? The first time doing this, you might feel very self-conscious, so make sure you have privacy, put the song or aria on repeat, and spend the next five to ten minutes in motion. Watching various dancers is also a great way to see how music makes people move. Expand your comfort zone and watch ballet, tap, modern, hip-hop, jazz, rap, and others. See how people move to the music.

And finally, know your orchestration. The timbre/color of the instruments will inform all that you do. Check out orchestra scores and see what is written. Listen to recordings and notate what instruments you are hearing. It is important to know, for example, that:

- The opening introduction of "Va! laisse couler mes larmes," from Massenet's *Werther,* is played by a saxophone, which continues through the aria.
- The melody line in "Una furtiva," from Donizetti's *L'elisir d'amore* is played by a bassoon.
- The introduction to Valentin's "O sainte médaille," from Gounod's *Faust* is played by trumpets and trombones.
- The introduction to "Quando me'n vo," from Puccini's *La bohème,* begins with clarinet, trades off to strings playing pizzicato, and then finishes with the harp.
- The piano vocal score does not usually indicate all of this, but in "Vecchia zimarra," from Puccini's *La bohème,* the flute or horn double the melody line at times.

- In Orlovsky's Couplet from *Die Fledermaus* by Johann Strauss, the introduction is orchestrated as follows: measure one, flutes and oboes playing forte, measure two, oboes and clarinets playing *forte*, measures three and four, the bassoons, horns, trombones, and strings playing *piano*.

All these color choices should inform what you, as the singer (aka soloist), will do.

Part 2.5

Activities to Deepen Your Practice

I find that most singers are creative people in general. The activities in this section are likely to appeal to that part of singers, young and old.

Recreate your aria "on stage"

For those of you who have been fortunate to sing your role or aria onstage with all the production values, you can reimagine the feeling. But even if you've never been on stage before, you can imagine it as well. Our imagination and resources these days are bountiful.

- Create a set, either by drawing, or finding a picture of what you envision the set to look like. You can find these online or in magazines. You're not limited by budget for your imaginary set.
- What props will you need? Start a props list and then source the props online or from magazines. If you have any of the objects in your home, or in the props shop at your school or local theater company, pick them up. What do they feel like? If you're sitting on a rock, you can get that sensation on a real rock. But on stage, the rock would be created just for you and will weigh very little but be reinforced to hold your weight. Volunteer in the local props shop to see how that magic is made.
- Create a costume for your character (again from magazines or online). What would they wear? Imagine what it would feel like to wear that costume. Are there whale bones in the corset or plastic? What do knickers and tights feel like, and how do men pull them off? How do they stand? How do they walk? Often, in opera, you will have a dresser to help you into and out of your costume. In addition to efficiency, this is also because the costumes are often very complicated to get into and out of.
- Give yourself a wig. Is your hair supposed to be long and flowing? Or perhaps a 30-pound wig will be piled on your head? Do you know how to pin curl your own hair to accommodate the layers that will be on top? What are the layers on top? You need to know!

A few notes

- If you are singing a song, you can approach it the same as if it were an aria. For example, in Schubert's "Die Forelle" you can get pictures of the trout steam, the fisherman, and the river. There are no boundaries to your imagination except those you self-impose.
- You might need to do some research on the costumes, sets, wigs, and props of the character you are portraying. Losing yourself in a google search, or in the stacks of books in an art library can be lots of fun.

Stage your aria or song

You can choose to go to a stage director or dramatic coach for this important task, or you can choose to stage your aria or song yourself. The objective is to give yourself a physical space and direction for what your character will do. I've seen this done in living rooms, rented classrooms, church basements, stages, and large rehearsal halls. You can do this work anywhere. But you truly do need to know where everyone and everything is in the piece you are singing. That will give you a specificity that is necessary for successful communication in your performance.

Keep a scrapbook

Your scrapbook might be physical or online and should explore the architecture and artwork from the period of your aria or song. What do the buildings look like? How do they differ from other time periods? In Mozart's *Le nozze di Figaro,* the Count and Countess have separate bedrooms. Is that a shocker, or is it simply the way it was done back then? I find artwork from the Impressionist era especially helpful when singing French *mélodies.* Let it inspire you and help you see what the *mélodie* is about.

Watch a ballet

You can choose to go in person and get caught up in the excitement that only a live audience can create, or you can look online. See how the dancers use their bodies to tell the story of the music. You can also watch modern dance, jazz, hip-hop, tap, and all the other mediums to help get physically inspired. It is all wonderful homework that helps you create a specific world around your repertoire and character.

Watch a full opera, or scenes from an opera

See what the largest (biggest budget) companies produce, but also see what scrappy, creative, innovative upstart opera companies can muster. You need to set eyes on live productions as often as possible. YouTube is a wonderful resource. You also can find less expensive alternatives for live performances such as student tickets (in NYC, for example, pre-pandemic the Metropolitan Opera as well as Broadway had student tickets at $35.00), standing room, rush tickets, lawn seats for outdoor venues, and the like. And, please, watch productions from the 1950s, or earlier, as well. How have our styles and tastes changed? You will also find productions of opera that are rarely roduced today.

Self-assess

This is a critical element. Notice that I didn't write *criticize yourself,* which is counterproductive. But self-assessment is a valuable tool. I believe that creating journals, notebooks, blogs (even if just for yourself), or diaries are key. What sort of journals are helpful? Here are a few that I particularly like:

- YES! Book. This is a notebook filled ONLY with positive things about you, your singing, and your progress. You fill the content with what people say to you that is positive as well as your own assessment of what you did well. For example, "My teacher said that I really seem to understand the technical concepts we've been working on in the passaggio of this aria." Or "The judge told me I have an incredibly beautiful, warm sound." Or "I feel like this audition was my best yet! Here's why..." We all have feelings of doubt or insecurity from time to time. The YES! Book will help you get through those days when you doubt yourself and/or your talent.
- Practice journal. This is a journal with detailed notes as to how your practice is going. This will help you, over time, realize what seems to work best for you in the most consistent manner in learning your repertoire. It can also help you identify your pitfalls.
- Audition journal. This details all the information about your auditions. Date, time, place, company, repertoire, panel, waiting room environment, warm-up space, acoustics in the room, pianist, piano quality, etc. This could (and likely should) include things like, how much sleep did you get, what time did you wake up, how did you get to your

audition, if by car, how easy was parking, if by train, how easy was it to find the subway to the venue or walk to the venue, etc. This way, over time, you will know exactly what to expect when you have an audition in city X, building Y, space Z.

Emotion cards

As indicated earlier in the book, you will create 300-400 (or more) 3x5 cards on which you will write one emotion (usually adjectives and adverbs, but it can be verbs as well). You can practice your text alone or in singing by using these cards to help you.

Text cards

Again, as indicated earlier in the book, you will write your texts, one sentence per card, or less if it is a very long sentence, and practice the texts. You can put five cards in your pocket, backpack, purse, or notebook each day. When you are walking somewhere, pull out a card to practice, silently and out loud, the text on that card. When you go to fill up your water bottle, pull out a card and practice that phrase all the way to the water fountain and back. When you are in a car pull out a card at a traffic light when it is safe to do so and see what is on that card. Keep practicing that phrase until you get to the next traffic light. You get the idea. It is spontaneous practice, a minute or two at a time, while you are doing something else.

Visualize your performance

Our minds are incredible tools. By creating a mental image of your performance, you can create the optimal performance of your repertoire. This is called visualization and helps stimulate the same brain regions that are affected when you are singing. Find a quiet space, close your eyes, and see/hear in your mind your performance, from walking out on stage (or the audition room), to handing the music over to your pianist, to announcing your name and musical selection, to breathing, to hearing the entire introduction, to singing the entire piece. If the song takes three minutes, this exercise will likely take four minutes. It is a commitment to yourself to perform the piece fully in your mind, how you want it to be, how terrific it can be. I suggest this for auditions, recitals, juries, recordings, opera roles, in fact any performance opportunity. For example, prior to your recital, it is not practical to sing your recital out loud every day. But you can sing your recital every day for the three weeks prior by choosing when to sing out loud and when to visualize. This helps in so many ways as your subconscious mind pairs with your conscious efforts to attain the musical and performance goals to which you aspire. You'll be surprised and pleased at how much work you can get done with visualization.

Part 2.6

Other Non-Singing Activities

By this point, you are likely thinking, "Is there really more that can be done?" The answer is: Absolutely. These ideas can help you with your creativity, your intellect, your knowledge, and your "package" as a performing artist. Ready?

Research new opera and songs to add to your repertoire

This is easy to do. There is so much new repertoire out there. The question is how to begin. The organization Opera America has a database of new American works that can be a good starting point. You can also do a google search of various opera companies to see what repertoire is in their season. Look at the singers in the production. Is there someone who typically sings the repertoire that you do? Check out the role that they are singing. Develop a working vocabulary of new operas, composers, librettists, companies that produce new opera so that you can jump into a conversation (or at least keep up!) that involves new work. Keep track of your research so that you always can refer to it. (See Appendix for many suggested resources.)

Research opera companies, summer programs, and competitions

Where might you find an opportunity? You'll never know unless you do some research. Check out opera companies, summer programs, competitions, and a plethora of other options. You can check Opera America, YAP Tracker, University/College programs, and opera company websites, as well as magazines like *Opera America, Opera News,* and *Classical Singer.* You can use your network of teachers, coaches, and colleagues. And remember to keep a notebook or spreadsheet of all your research so you won't have to repeat it in the future.

Paperwork

It is necessary, even if we don't like to do it and even if it is no longer *really* on paper. The following are key activities to help you move forward with your singing.

- Start or update your resume, which every singer needs. This should be a one page, clearly organized document that represents a fifteen second advertisement of your achievements. Again, Opera America has a free template on their website. I encourage you to copy that format exactly. Spelling counts (including accents, umlauts, and other diacritical marks).
- Write or update your 250-word bio. Where to start? Read the bios of other singers to see what is included. If you're not a very good writer, ask a friend to help you. Perhaps you could cook dinner for them in exchange. Find something that will benefit you both. Make sure your bio is written using correct English, without slang, or shortcuts.
- Create your repertoire list template.
    - When you sing an audition, you are usually required to bring a repertoire list of what selections you will be offering. When creating your template be sure to match the top of your list to the top of your resume. This should include your name, contact information and photo. This way, if your resume is lost, they still know how to contact you. (I suggest the same for the bio). The standard form is a list, well organized, with the following information: Composer, title of the Opera *in Italics,* name of the aria in quotation marks and normal typeface. These should be in three

  columns. Once you have the template, you can change out the repertoire as you need, but you've done the work of organization!
  - If you are offering a repertoire list for a jury or competition, you will need to see what the specific requirements are for that institution or organization. Please follow their instructions exactly, as they have pre-determined what materials they need from you.
  - Create a repertoire list to track all the repertoire you have studied, which must be kept up to date. You will need the following information.
    - Composer
    - Name of work (in italics if it is an opera or song cycle)
    - Role (if the work is opera or musical theater)
    - Language
    - Performed or prepared
    - If performed, you need to include
      - Company
      - Conductor
      - Stage Director
      - Dates (month and year)
- Start your audition diary/journal, your practice journal, or your YES! book. It doesn't matter if you use a physical or digital format; what is important is that you start it and keep up with it.
- Write a mission statement for who you are as a singer. Much like a company or other institution, you must know your mission. Read the mission statements of several opera companies and other not for profit organizations, which will give you a clue as to the typical content. Your mission statement should only be a few sentences long.
- Write a vision statement for who you are and want to be as a singer. Once again, you can find the vision statements for many companies online. You can make this a few sentences, a paragraph or two, or bullet points. The objective is for you to look ahead and see who you would like to be, what you would like to be doing, and how you would like to be doing it.

Reach out to others

Reach out to other singers in chat groups to discuss how your home practice is going or how your audition season is going. Get tips from each other, share successes as well as information about what you are still working on, and connect with college friends, even if you graduated years ago. Connect with singers with whom you've worked. I find, in general, that singers are social and very friendly. You will find *your* people. Help each other out.

Breathe

It is so important to take time out to breathe deeply. I will take a one-minute breathing break at various times throughout the day to help me settle and cleanse. Set your timer for one minute. Close your eyes and breathe in deeply through your nose and breathe out slowly through your mouth. When the gnats of the outside world fly through your thoughts, just swat them away and concentrate on the rhythm of your breathing. I think you'll be surprised at how terrific you feel after just one minute. Repeat as often as needed throughout your day.

Part 3: Application of Practice Tools A.K.A. Time to Play!

Part 3.1

Setting and Achieving Daily Goals

Sometimes, getting ready to practice can be overwhelming. You have so many options—where do you begin? If you don't purposefully plan your practice session, you might be led to procrastination, mindless repetition, or practicing too many things at once without improvement. Practice time is the perfect opportunity to perfect one thing at a time.

Setting—and achieving—daily goals for time

One of the keys to practice success is setting and achieving daily goals; If you write them down, you are more likely to hold yourself accountable. You know your schedule best. If you are a full-time student or work full time, it is highly unlikely that you can practice for eight hours a day. What is reasonable for you? (And by this time, you know that "practice" comes in many forms, not just singing.)

Keeping a practice journal is a good, tangible way to help keep you on track. If you have a close friend who is a singer, perhaps you can help hold each other accountable by sharing practice goals for the day as well as achievements.

Look at your calendar. Be specific about what time you will begin your practice each day of the week, and what time you plan to finish your practice Too often, "I'll practice later this afternoon," ends poorly when, at 8:00 pm, you realize that you haven't yet practiced. For example, perhaps you know that your warm-up time is 10:00 - 11:00 a.m. and your other pocket of time is 4:00 - 6:00 p.m. In that case, reserve this time for yourself for as long as you maintain that schedule.

Here is a sample. At the end of the day, you will have devoted four and a half hours to your craft. If your weekends are free, I suggest practicing for six to eight hours one day and taking the other day off to rejuvenate. Remember that a six to eight-hour practice day is not all about singing!

- 9:30 - 10:30 Warm up
- 10:30 - 3:30 Work or school
- 4:00 - 6:00 Practice (this is likely when you will do most of your singing)
- 6:00 - 7:30 Dinner
- 7:30 - 9:00 Practice (this is likely when you will do most of your non-singing work)

See Appendix for a template for a practice journal or plan.

Make your practice schedule SMART

- Specific
- Measurable
- Attainable
- Realistic
- Timely

Part 3.2

Identifying What to Practice

Where to start and what to do

In setting your goals, you will need to review what you are working on and identify places in your repertoire to practice. This needs to be specific, such as:

- I need to work on clarity in my sixteenth note runs in piece A
- I need to work on the text for velocity (with metronome) in piece B
- I need to make sure the arpeggios in this section are clean and in the center of the pitch
- I need to practice the performance of piece C in the shoes I will be wearing for the recital
- I need to translate the text of piece D
- I need to spend time listening to ten recordings of piece E
- I need to spend time visualizing my aria (audition package, recital)

And the list goes on. The work you do and the goals you set will change from time to time. And Parts 1 and 2 of this book provide you more practice ideas than you can do in one week, so each week can be slightly different to help ensure your practice remains *mindful* at all times.

You might find it helpful to develop a practice routine, such as warm-up in the morning, singing work in the afternoon, and non-singing work in the evening.

During audition season, I suggest practicing the opening measures of each of your audition selections at least once a day. This must be mindful work. It would also be a good idea to practice starting your auditions pieces at other points, in the event the auditors ask for that. For example, starting at the B section and then going to the ornamented A section of a *da capo* aria, or starting a longer aria at the cabaletta or after the accompanied recitative. You don't want a request to throw you off your game because you were not prepared for it. The same holds true for voice exams, recitals, and other non-operatic solos.

Most people start at the beginning of the phrase, especially if it is long. This practice often works well, but why not also try starting toward the end of the phrase? Make sure the phrase is exactly how you want it to be without worrying about running out of breath. For example, if a phrase is eight measures long, you might want to start on measure six, and hold the eighth measure for as long as you comfortably can. After doing this several times, start at measure five, repeating the process, followed by measure four, then three, two, and finally the beginning of the phrase. This way, you have concretized how the phrase needs to end with plenty of air, musicality, and confidence.

This also applies to the end of an aria or song. Sing the last page or two at the beginning of your practice when you are fresh. If you always sing from the beginning to the end, your body will remember: "Oh, we always get tired here, so we'll do it again this time." Muscle memory does not know what is good and what is bad. It only knows what you tell it to do most of the time. Break old habits, make the tough stuff easier, be successful with your musical goals.

It is important to practice for your performance in actual performance conditions. Put on your recital/audition shoes, put on your recital/audition attire and practice from start to finish. Keep going. Do not let mistakes derail this crucial step. And record this practice. You can listen later to remember what your next practice week needs to look like. But be and stay in the moment as if you are performing. If this is a recital, hear the applause, take your bow, and walk in and out as you plan to for the real thing.

I suggest running your recital (or audition or jury repertoire) daily for several weeks leading up to the actual date. WAIT, you say: “I won’t have learned all my music the month before,” or “It is impossible for me to sing my full recital every day.” Not to worry. We don’t expect the impossible.

You should have your music completely memorized by the month before your recital. If you do not, you have planned poorly. Why do that to yourself? Advanced planning, with a practice plan, will help you achieve that goal.

Regarding singing the recital each day, I encourage you to sing the recital out loud two or three times a week, depending on your schedule, the length of your recital, and the demands of the repertoire. The other three or four days you will sing the entire recital in your mind. This is the visualization that is presented in Part 2. You close your eyes and get comfortable. If your recital contains 50 minutes of music and a ten-minute intermission, your visualization will take *the same amount of time*. Picture the audience and venue. Hear the applause. Hear the hush before the pianist begins the opening selection. Sing your heart out, in your mind. Of course, the same practices apply to singing opera roles, concerted works, and other solo ventures. This method will help give you the confidence to sing your performance out loud on the actual date, as you’ve been practicing this for an entire month. Go forth!

Part 3.3

Soprano Examples

During my coaching sessions, singers often present the same or similar difficulties, which might be related to pitch, rhythm, text, phrase direction, or interpretation. Fortunately, there are solid practice solutions for making corrections. Please refer to your piano/vocal score when reading this section.

Mozart, *Die Zauberflöte,* "Ach, ich fühl's"

Harmony

My colleagues in the theory department will likely be both thrilled and mortified that I include this in the practice portion. When I say analyze, I do not mean the detailed analysis that we learn in college, even though that is terrific. I say analyze to see and feel what the intent of the composer might be.

This aria is in the key of G minor, which is noted clearly by the melody and harmony in measure one. The sixteenth note C_5 on beat six is a passing tone, but things start to shake up on the downbeat of measure two where the music shifts to G major with the added seventh in the accompaniment. The appoggiatura from A_4 to G_4 is the ninth of the chord. This dissonance to resolution exemplifies Pamina's pain and anguish. You find this again on the downbeat of measure three with the appoggiatura. Go through the aria and determine which pitches are passing tones and which are *appoggiature* (or appogiaturas. The root of appoggiatura is *appoggiare*, which means *to lean*. You will musically lean on the note, giving it more prominence in the melodic line. For example, the two note phrases on beats four, five, and six in measure thirteen are all *appoggiature*.

When Mozart includes an unusual harmonic progression, such as in measures seven and eight, listen to what your ear is expecting and what you hear. This is a musical and dramatic moment to note even if you are not singing, as it gives you more information about Pamina and her thoughts before temporarily modulating to the relative major key, B♭. At the end of the aria (the last nine measures), there is a series of false finishes on the tonic, the first being the downbeat of measure 33. Had Mozart chosen a G-minor chord at that moment, the aria could be over, but he had other thoughts in mind. Be a super sleuth and try to figure out what that could have been. For me, the $A\flat_4$ on the downbeat of measure 32 is the moment where she realizes death is her only answer, even though she said the word in measure 26. But that time it was on a pitch in the tonic triad, so it went largely unnoticed musically. Measures 33 and most of measure 34 create a loop that, had Mozart not shifted on beat six of measure 34, could have gone on endlessly. That is something to recognize as this occurs with Pamina's preparation and actualization of her high, pianissimo G_5. Measure 36 could also be the conclusion of the aria, as well as measure 37. But no, Mozart had something else in mind. When you get to the fermata in measure 37, Mozart wrote out exactly what he wanted sung. (There are many other Mozart arias where the fermata stands alone and performance practice suggests you add ornaments, but in this case, it is important to sing as Mozart wrote.) Notice in measure 38 the singer has a quarter note while the orchestra has an eighth note, followed by an empty beat three. Some of Mozart's most exquisite writing occurs after that for three and a half more measures. You should have a wonderful time analyzing this postlude!

Scales

Whether slow and subtle, like the G-minor descending scale in the first two measures, or a bit faster like the scalar passage in measure fourteen, scales are everywhere in this aria. Use the Five Daily Practice Tools on a regular basis and measure fourteen will be less threatening. This slow melisma functions as a simple F-major scale, used in a cadential $I^{6/4}$ to V^7dominant in the temporary key of B♭. Whether you use solfège or pitch names, it is important to keep the half and whole steps of this scale passage in tune, which, unfortunately, is a common pitfall for many sopranos.

Drama

What is Pamina trying to say? Reviewing the harmonic choices helps, but we also need to investigate what she is saying and why. She doesn't understand why neither Tamino nor Papageno will speak to her. Measures one through sixteen take us through the first section of her realization and misery. In measure seventeen, she approaches Tamino and directly confronts him with "See, Tamino, these tears flow for you alone." Certainly, that will get a reaction from her love. But no, no reaction. So, Mozart dots a rhythm in measure 22, to shake him out of his stupor on the text "don't you feel." Still no response, so she sings it again, but higher, this time on the G_5 in measure 27. I call this Pamina's "mini-mad scene," which is, stylistically speaking, appropriate. Puccini's Tosca jumps off the roof. Bellini's and Donizetti's women descend into madness worthy of fifteen minutes or more of exquisite singing in *I Puritani* and *Lucia di Lammermoor* respectively. What do Mozart's two measures of a dotted sixteenth note followed by a 32nd tell us about Pamina? This is where you get to choose. But it is there. The clues for us to pick up on are there.

Arpeggios

Yes, arpeggios are everywhere, too, which is why the Five Daily Musical Tools are key to everything. For Pamina, it starts with a simple G-minor arpeggio in second inversion in measure five, with an appoggiatura on beat six, the C♯$_5$ resolving to D_5. We continue the arpeggio in measure thirteen beginning on the third and stretching to the seventh and ninth before a resolution that is another appoggiatura. These arpeggios must be in tune. Practice them slowly and carefully so that you know exactly where those pitches are in your body and voice. When I play the piano, I can feel the arpeggios, but I can also see them. Singers don't have the luxury of "seeing" the arpeggios in their voice, but they can feel and know exactly where those pitches are. If you are having difficulty with a skip, just look at the harmonic structure and see where the skip fits in an arpeggio.

Breath

Breath, the source from which it all stems. This aria requires amazing breath control. If your singing teacher approves, I suggest lip or tongue trills to get used to the tessitura and range and length of the phrases. Once that feels comfortable and you successfully can navigate the phrases, choose your favorite vowel, or one that is more closed, like /o/ or /u/ or a vowel with an umlaut. These vowels can help you snake your way through the melody gently until you are ready to use the text.

Text
Always begin by speaking the text as a story or monologue with meaning and as close to native inflection as possible. Once you are truly comfortable with the text, speak it gently in rhythm, using a metronome to keep your tempo steady. Once you have achieved that, sing the text in rhythm on one pitch (no metronome when you sing). Eventually choose pitches that are in the same tessitura as the phrase so that you are closer in the ballpark of where you need to be to sing the aria.

Gounod, *Roméo et Juliette*, "Je veux vivre"

Half steps and number of notes to sing
The opening measures of this beautiful aria are tricky. First, you need to know how many notes you sing. Too often, this phrase is simply a slide down, with fingers crossed that you land on a pitch close to the B♭$_4$ The first measure is preparatory; practice it slowly, mid-tempo, and fast. Leave out the grace notes at the beginning, and then add them once you know exactly where the half step from C$_5$ to B$_4$ is in your voice. Start your count on the B♭$_5$. You can choose to count to thirteen, knowing that the last four notes are longer than the quarter notes. Or you can choose to count in smaller bundles: 123_123_123_1_2_3_4. Either way I encourage you to mark your score and count so you know where everything is supposed to line up. With the half steps, practice four at a time, focusing on the center of the pitch and intonation. Tapas sized portions are best for intense concentration Once you have secured all the pitches with spot-on intonation, you can begin expanding to include more notes. Be sure to practice at a variety of tempi.

Legato and line when there are rests (with and without grace notes)
Oftentimes the melody gets choppy here because of the rests. How do you achieve line in something like this? For practice, it is good to eliminate both the rests and the grace notes. The music clearly is felt as one beat per bar, but that tends to encourage choppiness. So, think of the first four measures as a measure of four. The second four measures are the second measure of four, and so forth. If you sing those eight measures on your best vowel, phrasing as if it is one long phrase, you should feel the momentum on beats three and four, leading you to the next strong beat, which helps you with the shape of the line. After you feel confident with that, add the rests back in, but keep the line going. This helps with your vocal GPS, the direction of the line. Simultaneously, sing the grace notes and the down beats. Notice the distance of the half and whole steps? Start slowly and gradually increase the speed of your grace note. Repeat each one eight times before moving on to the next so that you reinforce the place where the grace note and half steps/whole steps live. Use this practice tool for all the four measure phrases in the aria

Eighth-note runs
Eighth-note runs can be a pesky problem for intonation, accuracy, and tempo. Using the rhythms found in Part 1, explore the eighth-note phrases. Let's use the chromatic scale in the middle of the aria as an example. Again, in small chunks, begin your work with the first five notes: dotted eight and sixteenth notes, then sixteenth and dotted eighth notes, then quarter note and sixteenth note triplets, then sixteenth note triplets and quarter note. Start on any note in the four-measure phrase. Eventually, you will work on them all. By starting on any of the notes, you are working the half steps independently and will engrain where they belong in your voice. Too often this phrase becomes more of a slide and that throws

off the tempo, accuracy, and intonation. In most of the other eighth-note phrases, you will want to do this exercise with seven notes so that you are working the whole measure with each rhythm. It is always important to build a bridge to the next sequence.

Skips and intervals

There is an octave skip both down and up on the text *Cette ivresse*. Oftentimes the sixteenth note sounds more like an indistinct sound than an actual pitch. First, practice out of time and rhythm. Use portamenti both up and down on that octave until you know exactly where it belongs in your voice. Next, shift the rhythm to three equal quarter notes followed by dotted quarter note, eighth note, quarter note, and finally, the rhythm as written, double dotted quarter note, sixteenth note, quarter note. Each of these exercises should be practiced for several minutes with complete success before moving on to the next. This could happen in fifteen minutes, or over the course of several days. It matters not the length of time it takes for success, only that you are successful.

Another difficult skip is the sixth in the next to last set of runs before the final set and the difficulty of the A_5 to C_5 (I can almost see sopranos nodding their heads in agreement). Oftentimes, even if the first one is accurate, each subsequent A sags in pitch, or the C inches up and rides high on the pitch. Again, using the portamento, find the distance between the two pitches. This time practice the sequence as five quarter notes. When that is secure, move to five eighth notes, then use the rhythm of the dotted eighth note and sixteenth note, and then the reverse, the sixteenth note and dotted eighth note. Another good practice tool here is to sing one measure and one pitch, putting a fermata on the high A so that you can make sure it is in tune and in the right place. Or sing the seven notes, putting a fermata on the sixth note.

Move your body

So, with all this difficult musical and technical work, it is crucial to keep your body supple and free. I suggest dancing to the music. First, without singing. What does your body want to do, how does it want to sway? Then dance while singing. Move your arms, let the music take over. With a released body, it is very difficult to hold tension in other body parts that are key to singing.

Puccini, *La bohème,* "Quando me'n vo"

Tempo

It is super important to choose your tempo wisely. Puccini indicated ♩ = 104, but most singers and conductors now take it slower. However, if you get the chance to listen to the Toscanini recording for RCA, broadcast in 1946, you will note that the tempi for everything are more in line with the metronome suggestions in the score. Since Toscanini conducted the world premiere, I hold great credence that this Maestro knew just what he was doing. However, if it feels too fast for you, a click or two less on the metronome will be fine. Just please don't turn it into a dirge.

The next thing is to know when the music is in tempo and when there is a change (*quasi rit, appena allarg, rit. molto, molto rall, poco rall., rit., rall., poco allargando*). I suggest that once you are comfortable and accurate with the text, speak it the rhythm and tempo of the aria, but take it one step further; make the *a tempo* quite brisk and the changes (which all slow the tempo down) very slowly. This way, you know precisely where the changes occur with the text. Please don't rely on the pianist to lead you through these changes (you should be leading them!). You want *your own* stamp on the aria, not your *pianist's.*

Music and dramatic shape

I like to think of this aria in the shape of a funnel. The first verse is addressed to everyone. The aria, of course, is sung by Musetta, a confident woman who makes *soletta* feel charming by the closed /e/ and the double /t/, and who knows that when she says *ricerca, she* is not relooking, but rather everyone else is gazing at her beauty.

I like to think of the second part, *ed assaporo allor,* as a secret amongst the men she has taken as lovers. It is secret and mysterious. And even has a *When Harry Met Sally* moment in the *felice mi fa.*

The third verse is to the one she truly loves, Marcello, *E tu che sai.* She calls him out on his feelings. And he knows she's right and can't even bear to look at her.

This simple funnel helps give specific focus to each verse.

Orchestration

Who is playing in the orchestra? You need to know because it informs your choices. For example, the three repetitions of an eighth note B♮ before *Quando me'n vo* are played by the harp. What does a harp sound like? Where else is the harp prominent? I can assure you it appears much more than the typical piano vocal score indicates. Be grateful for the sage pianist who has taken the time to do the research and write in the extra harp parts. And when Puccini writes *pianissimo* it is often accompanied by full orchestra, which is a different kind of feel than the *pianissimo* of a solo instrument. So, make sure you know what is playing with you by consulting the orchestra score or using your ears to identify the instruments on a recording.

Arpeggio and the B_5 at the end

Be sure that you practice that E-major arpeggio at the end so that you can nail it each time, using the various ways to practice that are in Part 1 as well as in the examples above. The final B_5 must decrescendo but still have lots of energy leaving the pitch as she delivers her punchline to Marcello.

Pesky passages

Verdi, *Falstaff,* "Sul fil d'un soffio etesio"

The first note that the soprano sings on each of the two verses (as well as two measures later) needs a note of caution. While the piano/orchestra has a triplet feeling with their groupings of six sixteenth notes, the singer must come in with a duple eighth note. Practice this with only the duple feel, tapping the duple beat. Speak and sing this crucial rhythm multiple times a cappella. Then back up and think quarter notes for the ¾ time signature, which is how conductors navigate that tempo. You can continue your duple beat pattern so that you see how it fits into the orchestra part. In woodworking, it is suggested that one measures twice and cuts once. In this pesky part, listen many times, get used to the feel of where your duple comes in. Then you can sing!

Menotti, The Old Maid and the Thief, "Steal me"

The meter at the beginning of the aria proper is 7/8: too many singers unintentionally omit beat seven, which is occupied by the word *Oh.* Set your metronome to a comfortable tempo, using the eighth note as the beat (♪ =120 is a good tempo). Count to seven with the metronome. Note that *Steal* occupies beats one and two, *me* occupies beats three, four, five, and six, and then *Oh* has the entirety of beat seven. This also occurs at rehearsal number 99 with the text *death comes and.* Please don't omit this beat.

Mozart, *Le nozze di Figaro,* "Deh vieni non tardar"

Sometimes vowel clusters can be difficult and often a singer will just choose to omit a vowel. Please do not do this, especially in this aria with the phrase, *finchè l'aria è ancor.* Per the score, the following consonants and vowels should be sung on beat five on the pitch G: *ria è an.* It is a mouth full, yet it must be elegant, like this aria. Start with two vowels, */i_a/,* and repeat them fluidly in your mouth; move to */a_è/* and do the same thing; and then */è_a/* and—surprise—it is the same as the */a_è/*—two for the price of one practicing! Then shift to three vowels */i_a_è/* repeating them fluidly and gaining in speed. Then */a_è_a/,* doing the same thing. Then add the consonants so that you have the full */ria_è_an/.* In addition to speaking this combination, sing it on a pitch of your choosing. Then change pitches. The objective is to make it comfortable in your mouth as you sing. One you are comfortable with that, sing beats four, five, and six, first on any vowel/consonant combination, like *lu.* Then add the text *l'aria è ancor. L'a* is on beat four, */ria_è_an/* is on beat five, and *cor* is on beat six. Repeat frequently, as this is a stumbling block for many singers.

Puccini, *La bohème*, "Donde lieta"

There is often a bump or awkward tempo/rhythm moment in this iconic aria in the fourth measure when singing the phrase *torna sola Mimi.* To understand and control the tempo as the music shifts to 3/4 at the Andantino, it is important to subdivide. The aria begins in 2/4 but is conducted and felt as if it were in 4/4, with the eighth note getting one beat. At *torna sola Mimi,* shift to six, feeling the beat on the eighth note, which many conductors do as well. This gives you great control and clarity as you sing the upbeat to the new tempo.

Mozart, *Die Zauberflöte*, "Der Hölle Rache"

In general, be careful how you start this aria, as putting too much weight and heft on the opening can compromise what comes later. Also, arpeggio work abounds in this aria, so please pay attention to the arpeggios by practicing them daily and using the exercise found in Part 1. In your daily practice, make sure your arpeggios go into the stratosphere like they do in this aria. Intonation is super important as is knowing exactly where those pitches are in your voice and body. But two of the trickiest parts of a very difficult aria are the repeated notes and the triplets.

With the repeated pitches, singers often migrate higher and thinner on each one. I suggest practicing the repeated notes by starting with only three. When those are secure, sing four. Then five, etc. until you can sing all eight. I would be an overachiever, if I were you, and sing twelve if possible. Then eight seems easy. After you are secure with the repeated notes, add beat four preceding them, first without the grace note, and then, after much successful practice, with the grace note. When you add the four sixteenth notes of beat four, it might be wise to only sing three or four of the repeated notes, until you make sure they remain in the correct place. Otherwise, you will quickly undo the amazing practice before you added the sixteenth notes. In measures 29-31, think smaller units by only practicing five notes at a time, the first five eighth notes, and then move on to beats three and four, building the bridge to the first note of measure 30, and so forth. These tapas sized practice bites allow for success and stability quicker than trying to do it all at once.

At measure 69 there are those pesky triplets. As indicated in Part 1, it is helpful to sing the backbone of the triples once or twice (F, A, F, D, C♯, etc.) so that you know clearly what the outline is. Now, for work on the triples, practice by lengthening the middle note of the triplet and by accenting the middle note of the triplet at a reduced tempo. Practice at many tempi. When you are ready to increase your speed to *a tempo* you may eliminate the accent, but the middle note should stay securely in place. Triplets are often a lifetime of work for singers.

Mozart, *Die Zauberflöte*, "O zittre nicht"

In addition to all the practice tools for the other arias, this fiendish aria includes measured trills. (As does Konstanze in *Die Entführung aus dem Serail.*) I suggested revisiting the five daily exercises in Part 1 as the half step measured trill in measure 91. Too often, the singer "flatlines" the trill and the two pitches are not distinguishable.

Also, don't forget the arpeggio and scale work found in Part 1!

Part 3.4

Mezzo Examples

During my coaching sessions, singers often present the same or similar difficulties, which might be related to pitch, rhythm, text, phrase direction, or interpretation. Fortunately, there are solid practice solutions for making corrections. Please refer to your piano/vocal score when reading this section.

Massenet, *Werther,* "Va! Laisse couler mes larmes"

Context

Before jumping in to tackle this amazing aria, it is important to know some context about its position in Act III, which takes place on Christmas Eve. Charlotte, deep in thought about Werther, rereads his letters to her and wonders how she had the strength to send him away. She is interrupted by her perky younger sister, Sophie, who sees that Charlotte is upset and, after a brief attempt to cheer her up, challenges her, claiming she's been despondent since Werther went away. This is where "Va! Laisse couler mes larmes" comes in. After the aria and a short exchange with Sophie about joining the family for the Christmas festivities, Charlotte sings another aria, asking God to hear her prayers and come to her aid. Werther suddenly returns and they have an extended, emotional scene, after which Charlotte runs out of the room, Werther flees, and Albert—Charlotte's husband—enters the empty room, having learned of Werther's return. He calls for Charlotte, who appears in a panic, which Albert notices. Werther has left a note to Albert explaining that he is leaving on a long voyage (which in this case is not a trip anywhere) and would like to borrow Albert's pistols. Albert insists that Charlotte herself give the guns to a servant to give to Werther. At the last minute, after a premonition, Charlotte races out of the room hoping to reach Werther in time to prevent the disaster. So, you see, Charlotte is onstage the entire time, and the singer must look at, study, and understand the entire arc of the scene to see where "Va!" fits in.

Charlotte is honor- and duty-bound to Albert in a way that was not uncommon in the 1800s, but her heart and soul belong to Werther. A terrific read that has a similar marriage imprisonment is Henrik Ibsen's play, *A Doll's House.*

Dynamic Shape and Rhythm

The first seven measures that Charlotte sings form a funnel of musical dynamics. "Va!" starts out *forte,* with a strong /v/ connected to the /a/ vowel. The text *Va! Laisse couler me larmes* is commanding, enhanced by the absence of accompaniment in that measure; the singer has control over the tempo, but also must maintain clear rhythm and tempo (absence of accompaniment does not mean a free for all!). The opening phrase quickly settles into a *piano* dynamic level for the phrase *elle font du bien.* Charlotte is releasing some of her pent-up emotion and showing affection for her sister. After measure eight, marked *très rallentando,* the orchestra is *triple piano,* which the singer must match. So, the overall arc is that the dynamics go from Charlotte's outburst insisting that it is okay to cry and have feelings, to explaining more gently that tears can be good, and almost apologizing to her sister by calling her "my dear," to singing from the depths of her soul about the internal trauma when one does not let the tears out. As she digs deep emotionally, the dynamics reflect the pain that she feels.

On the word *las*, be sure to color the crescendo with the text, weary/tired. Every dynamic has an important meaning in this aria.

The repeated F_4 of *et s'affaiblit* is marked tenuto with a decrescendo to *pianissimo.* The text and the harmony let us know there is more to come, but she is having a highly emotional moment in this phrase that allows us to wonder where she is going with this.

Before beginning the phrase *et trop fragile,* wait for the orchestra/piano to clear the chord, hear the octave D, and only then think about singing. This prepares you and the listener for the final phrase, which punctuates the aria with sorrow. It should be intimately sung, as Charlotte knows that her heart ultimately will break.

Articulation

There are two terrific exercises to reinforce articulation in this aria, which is crucial to its success. First, after having successfully spoken the text as poetry or a story, speak the text in rhythm, paying strict attention to the articulation. Second, sing the text in rhythm on one pitch, highlighting the articulation. Begin to marry the intent of the word (translation) with the intent of the articulation.

There are many tenuto markings in this aria that help you express the text. For example, at *sa résistance* and *enfin s'épuise*, the articulation helps convey the emotion of the text in the words. "Resistance" and "finally runs out" are hard for Charlotte to say, yet they are in a section of the aria where the tempo moves forward a bit. It is something essential for her to say, followed by *le cour se creuse... et s'affaiblit.*

Arpeggios

There are five sets of arpeggios that must be in tune and completely focused. Excerpt these arpeggios for independent work as described in the daily exercises in Part 1: 1) *les larmes qu'on,* 2) *et de leurs pa-*, 3) *il est trop grand,* 4) *rien ne l'emplit,* 5) *et trop fragi(le).* Three of them are on the same pitches, but the vowels are different, so each one needs unique attention. You need to know exactly where they live in your body and sound. It is also important to know and remember that the arpeggio for *et de leur pa(tiente)* leads to the higher register two measures later. This octave shift needs to be prepared with the breath before the singing even begins. A good way to practice this is to sing the F_5 with a *portamento* down to the D_5 at the beginning of the arpeggio in measure fifteen so that the entire phrase is informed by where it needs to end up. Eventually, after repetition of this exercise correctly, your breath and body will know what to do before you even begin to sing.

Line and Legato

This aria, despite the rests and articulation, is a study in line and legato. Note the long phrases, some of which include intermediate breaths. Practice the phrases on a vowel, with perfect legato binding the tones together and with a vocal GPS that matches Massenet's phrasing. Work on one phrase at a time, taking the time it needs to feel the shape of the phrase.

Mozart, *Così fan tutte,* "Ah scostati… Smanie implacabili"

Text

Fiorliligi's younger sister cannot imagine life without her betrothed, Ferrando, and throws a wild, musical temper tantrum! Dorabella is histrionic and uses words not in common Italian vocabulary, while making the recitative text still seem organic. The text must be practiced as a spoken dramatic piece. Use the notecards from Part 1 to help with attitudes.

When she opens with *Ah scostati*, it is not part of her vernacular speech; it is like us saying, "Ah, flee from here," or "Ah, move yourselves away." It is affected, but this girl or young woman is trying to express what she considers more mature feelings. She spies the open window and demands *Chiudi quelle finestre* (shut that window). It seems to me that if the window had been closed, she would have insisted just as vigorously that it be opened. She sees something and demands a change. Then she states that she hates the light, the air that she breathes, and (likely in Sarah Bernhardt fashion) that she even hates herself.

The text then takes a turn with "who mocks/scorns my sorrow… who consoles me…" The dramatic beat shifts with this text and slows down the mounting agitation, resembling, perhaps, a pity party.

Finally, she demands that Fiordiligi and Despina leave her alone with shorter, clipped phrases and the text *fuggi*, which is more in the vernacular of her regular speech and means, similarly to her opening text, flee/escape/leave/go away.

Musical Shape of the Recitative

After giving a chord to establish pitch and tonality, the singer should take time to motivate the opening phrase. Following *Ah scostati*, the orchestra/piano has a relatively unstable chord, an A major harmonic 7 chord in third inversion, which suggests Dorabella is unsure of how she's going to proceed. It is quickly followed by D-major and D-minor scales, which are much more harmonically predictable, perhaps prompting her to use what she has around her as an anchor. The "I hate" litany ends with a G-minor scale. The first violin begins a plaintive melody, usually at a slower tempo, that leads into *Chi schernisce il mio duol*. This change allows Dorabella to question who it is that mocks her sorrow, and who consoles her. The beginning of a B♭-major scale abruptly stops on the harmonic seventh, this time in second inversion, which pulls Dorabella out of her melancholy into her demanding to be left alone, accompanied by strong E♭-major chords in root position, before the final dominant/tonic cadence, again in root position, of F major and B♭ major. These are all clues as to what Mozart intended for this younger sister. Use your imagination to fill in the blanks so that your Dorabella is unique, but still follows the trail of Mozart's harmonic progressions.

Line and Legato

There are many challenges in this aria, and one of the first to address is the idea of line and legato. The line should not sound like a series of hiccups scattered throughout. I suggest singing four measure phrases without rest or breath. This is not the ultimate form your breath choice will take, but it is a great way to practice how to achieve a line and the illusion of legato even with the rests. At the same time, it is key to practice speaking the text in tempo and rhythm so that it is clear where the rests are and how to use them. (See the section on Tempo below.) Once you are comfortable with the four measure phrases, erase where the breaths are and sing the phrase with the same line, allowing for space during the rests. This is different from singing in a scalloped fashion where each beat pulls the line down. Allow measures four and five to help you swing the momentum to the next set of four measures (the same with measures eight and nine and so forth).

Arpeggios

Arpeggios are everywhere, which is why special attention is needed to ensure correct intonation and accurate musicianship. Look at the opening of this aria. Measures two and three are an arpeggio, just not in the 1, 3, 5 (*do–mi–sol*) fashion, but as 1, 5, 3. Measure four continues the trend of E♭ major, while measure five takes us through the first-inversion B♭-seven chord. Circle all the triads (checking for all the inversions) work on them independently so that you know exactly where they are in your voice, body, and in the aria. Practice on a vowel, then another vowel, then the vowels of the words where they occur, then finally on the text.

Tempo

As indicated in the above section about line and legato, it is important to practice speaking the text in tempo and rhythm. I suggest using a metronome when you speak so that a steady tempo becomes a habit. I also suggest starting at a much slower tempo, as referenced earlier in the book. Perhaps starting with the metronome set at 60 for the half note is a good place to begin. If that is too fast for 100% text accuracy (such as the vowel/consonant combination of *nieim* on beat two), slow it down even further. I also suggest eight measure phrases. It is better to repeat something accurately so that you can achieve mastery. Increase the metronome by twos (62, 64, 66, etc) until you get to about 80 or 90 beats per minute, when you can shift to increases by one. Only increase the tempo when you have achieved mastery, as previously noted. Increase the metronome until you get to 120, or for the bravest of souls, 140. Your language should always be legato. And this can be done *sotto voce* or gently so as not to stress your voice. That being said, it is still better to do this in three-to-five-minute chunks with a different practice activity in between.

On an unrelated note, but still in the realm of tempo, measure 90 is usually more successful if it begins *a tempo* after the breath. There is still the final stretch of singing, and broadening the tempo often adds an undesirable weight to the phrase and sound, making the end difficult.

Also, please be careful what you ask for. I was once instructed by a singer at an audition to "play this as fast as you can." In all humility, I can play that aria faster than any singer could ever sing it, so put a metronome number at the beginning so that the pianist knows your ballpark tempo, and then, if it is too fast or too slow, change it immediately the first measure you come in. If you wait to "see if it works" and then try to change it, we likely will interpret your efforts as rushing or dragging. Know your tempo and sing it. I can assure you that most pianists are on high alert for tempo changes after they've established your tempo.

Tessitura and Intonation

This aria sits high. I suggest practicing eight-measure phrases a half step higher and lower than written, which likely will make the key of E♭ major feel more comfortable to you. Some singers might want to practice the entire aria in E major. But you need to assess your comfort level and decide whether eight measure phrases are better than the whole thing.

Barber, *Vanessa,* "Must the winter come so soon?"

What's in the score and what's not

Who knew that this iconic aria was not in the original score of *Vanessa?* I think we're all glad that Ms. Elias had the courage to stand up for herself, and by consequence, all mezzos, as this aria is now a staple in the repertoire.

From *Opera News,* "Song of the Cold," written by Patrick Dillon, November 2013, Vol. 78, No. 5:

> "I was doing just small parts at the time," Elias recalls, "but when I heard that Sam and Gian Carlo were coming to hear me in *Butterfly*, I tried hard to make Suzuki the opera's leading role. No one seemed to hold that against me, though! They offered me Erika and sent me the score — and I went through every page and saw that everyone had an aria but me. So I went to Mr. [Rudolf] Bing — I don't know how I had the nerve to do this, but at that young age, you do! — and said, 'Mr. Bing, I love this opera, and I'm so honored to do it, but I'm the only character who doesn't have an aria.' Well, he picked up the phone and dialed and said, 'Hello, Sam, I have Rosalind Elias here, and she wants to talk to you' — and handed me the phone!" She repeated her plaint, as tactfully as she could, and, as she says, "That was it. He knew my voice by then, and I like to think he wrote this wonderful aria especially for me, it was so perfectly suited to me." Many years later, composer Lee Hoiby told Elias that he'd been at Barber's house when the call came in. "What an upstart!" he'd remarked when Barber put down the receiver.

The next thing to know is that the introduction that is ubiquitously heard in audition or recital performance is not what is in the score. It is beautiful and fitting, but when you learn this aria, you must consult the complete score. This aria appears just twenty pages into the opera and follows a conversation about the menu for Christmas, reading, the weather, and waiting. The mood of the house is one of constriction with Vanessa having locked herself down emotionally to the extent that all the mirrors in the house have been covered. Her mother, the Baroness, has been mute for twenty years and Erika is stuck in the upper northern territory with the two older women. It is fine to use this either when excerpting the aria with piano, or in an orchestra concert, but you need to know that it does not really start that way. That informs how you begin this haunting and touching aria.

Following rehearsal number sixteen, after the *forte* "Must the winter come so soon?," many excerpted piano/vocal editions add a full measure between the words "soon" and "here," which is neither in the orchestra score nor the piano/vocal score. It is important to know this and to eliminate the measure in your music if it is there.

Dynamics and tempo

The piano/vocal score is marked ♩ = 72, but I rarely have heard any singer sing it at that speed: It is frequently sung much slower (for example recordings of Frederica von Stade and Katherine Ciesinki). Nonetheless, I hold truth to the metronome marking if the composer put it there. It is a guidepost. However, in this instance, 72 does not lend itself to "Tranquil and sustained," which are the tempo indicators at the aria. Find a tempo that works for you throughout the entire piece (remembering the long phrase at the end). Your tempo might slow down a bit with experience and age as you have more control over your instrument.

The aria starts out *piano.* Soon, however, you will notice hairpins, a colloquial expression for a crescendo/decrescendo that is written into the music. For example, "Night after night, I hear the..." is a crescendo followed by a decrescendo on "hungry deer," so, this hairpin occurs over-two-and-a-half measures. The next phrase has the hairpin over six beats. These are important to highlight in your score (perhaps by using a red pencil or some other color that will get your attention). The first *forte* is at rehearsal sixteen, the restatement of "Must the winter come so soon?" You must determine why the dynamics and hairpins occur where they do. Give them dramatic reason. Make them count.

Onomatopoeia and alliteration

I love both these words. There is never enough opportunity to use them! Onomatopoeia is the imitation of a sound in the word. Easy examples are buzz and hiss. I think the word "hoots" in this aria is another great example. I can just hear that beautiful, haunting sound of the owl in that word.

Alliteration is the repetition of consonant sounds. The online dictionary, Merriam-Webster includes the description: "the repetition of [usually] initial consonant sounds in two or more neighboring words or syllables (such as wild and woolly, threatening throngs)." They abound at the beginning of this aria: hear/hungry, wander/weeping/woods, brittle/bark. How you treat them depends on several things. The /h/ in "hear" is easy to sing; the /h/ in "hungry" less so. But you can give the illusion to the alliteration and then, with a good second syllable, we will hear the alliteration quite clearly.

There is another measure that, to me, suggests the idea of onomatopoeia, not for the imitation of the sound, but for the length of the phrase. In the one and only statement, "It is a long winter here," Barber shifts from 4/4 to a unique measure of 3/2, which lengthens (draws out, elongates) that phrase. The listener doesn't necessarily know this is what is happening, but the singer certainly does because of the breath needed and the listener will hear the phrase as longer than usual.

Barber using the same melodic material in different works

I love that Samuel Barber quotes himself in his own music! He wrote the *Hermit Songs* in 1953 and *Vanessa* in 1958. "The Desire for Hermitage," the final song in the *Hermit Songs* opens with the melody, both in the piano and the voice "Ah, to be all alone," that is conjured up again in *Vanessa.* For a real treat listen to Leontyne Price, who sang the world premiere of the *Hermit Songs,* sing the entire set.

Breath control

The phrases in this aria are long, especially at the end. It is pretty common practice to breath before the word "so" four measures before the end. But still, that final phrase is twelve-and-a-half beats long! I suggest starting with the B♭. Get a great breath and sustain it for as long as you are able while still keeping a spinning sound. Practicing on a lip or tongue trill also is good for this exercise. If you are brave, after doing this several times, count the beats that you are holding the B♭. I find that singers can often hold that B♭ for sixteen beats or longer, which is three-and-a-half beats longer than is necessary for the phrase. After you have mastered that, add the eighth notes (A and C) before the B♭, and hold for as long as you are able, following the same sequence as on the B♭ alone. Once mastered, back up one more beat and do the same. Then back up another beat, etc. until you are at the breath before "so." This gives you significant practice time with the right breath and the right spin on the sound through the end of the phrase. It might be necessary to keep up this exercise with regularity for a while so that you keep that ending super solid.

Pesky Passages

Mozart, *Le nozze di Figaro,* "Non so più"

Like many Mozart arias, the tessitura sits high and singers have the tendency is to ride high on the pitch or even sing sharp. As mentioned with the "Smanie," I suggest practicing eight measure phrases both half step higher and half step lower than written, which likely will make the key of E♭ major feel more comfortable to you. Some singers might want to practice the entire aria in E major, but you need to assess your comfort level and decide whether eight measure phrases are better than the whole thing.

The introduction to this aria is quite short and usually a bit petrifying for the singer. You might want to ask your pianist to take a quick, audible breath through their nose as an ictus before they begin so that you know a full beat ahead of the downbeat. Another option is for the singer to breathe *with* the pianist, as if they started together. Singers consider the pianist at the end. Your breath before the final "parlo d'amor con me" needs to be obvious: If you sneak in, the end will be sloppy.

For some reason in this aria, singers frequently put a diphthong on the final vowels. Be attentive to that from the beginning so that you can sound authentically Italian

Mozart, *La clemenza di Tito,* "Parto, parto"

The opening pitches on the text *parto* are difficult for the singers and eye opening for coaches and teachers. I suggest practicing these regularly on closed vowels (perhaps even six to ten times each practice) with a portamento between the B♭$_4$ and F$_4$ and the C$_5$ and F$_4$. (Extending that to the *ma tu, ben mio* is also good for the octave skip down.) After your work with closed vowels, switch to more open vowels while keeping in mind the feel and place of the closed. Add the text only when you feel you can do this beautifully and correctly. It might also be helpful to sing *arto, arto* for a bit. The /p/ often compromises the vowel, so make sure you know just where that vowel is first.

Tempo is crucial in this piece. Pianists should subdivide, thinking sixteenth notes at the beginning of the introduction. It is also helpful for the pianist to think about the clarinet melody that is to come. At the *allegro* (second section), the singer has six measures to ascertain if the tempo is good for her. If it is, terrific. If not, you must change it on *Guardami e* by either shortening or lengthening the half note. It is important, in general, to know how to change a tempo on your first measure so that the musical choices are truly yours. Marking metronome indications is a great way to help the pianist take your tempo, otherwise, they are likely to play a tempo from their last singer or that they have played most frequently. The same holds true for the third section, *allegro assai.*

In the *Allegro assai* section, there are those pesky triplets. As indicated in Part 1, it is helpful to sing the backbone of the triples once or twice (B♭, D, C, E♭, D, F, *etc.*) so that you know clearly what the outline is. Now, for work on the triples, practice by lengthening the middle note of the triplet and by accenting the middle note of the triplet at a reduced tempo. Practice at many tempi. When you are ready to increase your speed to *a tempo* you may eliminate the accent, but the middle note should stay securely in place. Triplets can be difficult and often pose a lifetime of work for singers.

The last pesky problem is the arpeggios, starting with *ma tu, ben mio*, continuing with meco *ritorna in pace*, and continuing throughout the aria. Know where they are and use them in your daily practice so they can become a strength, rather than a liability.

Gounod, *Faust,* "Faites lui mes aveux"

Please refer to the first paragraph under Mozart, *Le nozze di Figaro*, "Non so più," as the same intonation issues apply here.

Additionally, think longer phrases in this aria to avoid the one measure choppiness that often occurs. If you think of it in four, the measure before you sing becomes beats one and two. The measure you begin becomes beats three and four. Continuing this thinking will help with the line and legato.

In telling the story in this aria, you need to dig back to Act 1 so that the middle section makes sense to you. You also need a complete inner life as to who Marguerite is to you.

And just when you think it is safe to sing this aria, please look at the "scene and recitative" immediately following the aria. There is a high $B\flat_5$ that follows a G_5 and A_5. This is a super difficult sequence. Be sure you can sing this before auditioning for the role. An astute General or Artistic Director will likely ask for that scene as well to make sure you are vocally secure in what comes after your aria.

Part 3.6

Tenor Examples

During my coaching sessions, singers often present the same or similar difficulties, which might be related to pitch, rhythm, text, phrase direction, or interpretation. Fortunately, there are solid practice solutions for making corrections. Please refer to your piano/vocal score when reading this section.

Donizetti, *L'elisir d'amore,* "Una furtiva lagrima"

Breath

Breath, the source from which it all stems. This aria requires amazing breath control. I suggest lip or tongue trills to get used to the tessitura and range, and length of the phrases. Once that feels comfortable and you successfully can navigate the phrases, choose your favorite vowel, or one that is more closed, such as /o/ or /u/, or a vowel with an umlaut. These vowels can help you snake your way through the melody gently until you are ready to use the text.

Carrying and Binding (aka *Portamento* and *Legato)*

A reminder on what legato means: the infinitive of the verb is *legare,* to tie, to bind, or to connect. In music, we connect through sound (thank you, John Wustman). The sound can be vowels and consonants, but there is always sound. And we keep the sound moving, spinning. In this aria, there are several *portamenti* written in or traditionally added, the first of which is found in the first two pitches, F_4 to $B\flat_3$. This is a great spot to use the arpeggio exercise. When working on this aria, especially in the beginning, I would suggest frequent use of the $B\flat_3$ as the "note for the day" (see Part 1). In general, *portamenti* should be light, little, and late. Going back to the Italian language, the word comes from the verb *portare,* to carry. What are we carrying? Sound. No need to belabor the sound and stretch it out too much. The accent on *lagrima* is in the context of the legato and line. Be sure to talk to your teacher about how to make an accent with your support rather than your consonants. The third measure has another delicious *portamento* from the $G\flat_4$ to the C_4 (a bit trickier for intonation as that is the tritone). After the *portamento* there is a subtle but very important double /c/ in the word *occhi* that can make us fall even more in love with Nemorino.

Language

Continuing from the paragraph above, with the next phrase *quelle festose giovani* there are a few language issues. The typical IPA transliteration suggests /kw/ as the first sound in *quelle*; however, the Italian alphabet does not include the letter /W/. I suggest that you move from the /k/ through the /u/ to /ɛ/, which will help avoid the spreading of the vowel that too frequently happens with words that begin with */qu/*. Spreading also must be avoided in the middle of *festose* on the $A\flat_4$: the closed /o/ actually is a perfect acoustic match for that pitch. /o/ also is your friend on the following word, *giovani.* Special attention must be given to the E_4, which often is sung flat. Those measures need more attention going from the G♭ to the E♮ several times, and then from the G♭ to the E, and then the F. Then backing up one note to start on the A♭ and singing the sequence. A good, though jarring exercise is to play block chords under the vocal line starting with B♭ minor, A♭ major seven, and replacing the D♭-major chord with a C-major chord, as it is easier to tune. Once you are secure in the E♮, it can be returned to its *appoggiata* state by playing the D♭-major chord. In reviewing the language of this soulful aria, it is especially important to attend to the beauty of the language, opening and closing the vowels correctly. For example, be sure to close the o in *non,* but open it in *può.*

Sounds Like a Sad Song

"Hey Jude" by the Beatles, had the right idea, "take a sad song and make it better." Although the aria is written in B♭ minor and opens with a plaintive melody from the bassoon, Nemorino is happy. Adina's secret tear leads him to the presumption that she loves him and he's so happy, hence the shift to the relative major, D♭, on the text, *M'ama* (she loves me). We hear the words and the emotion of shifting to the relative Major which allows the listener to feel the emotional shift as well. This happens in the second verse as well on the word *Cielo.* The intimacy of this aria can allow for little movement on the stage. In fact, the audience went wild after the aria when William Burden sang this aria entirely from a position sitting down on the lip of the stage the at the Academy of Music in Philadelphia (Opera Company of Philadelphia), which was spell-binding. This was before the internet and speedy communication, but word got out, and as the Director of Artistic and Music Administration for the Opera Company of Philadelphia, I was inundated with phone calls asking if it was truly as spectacular as they were hearing. The answer was simple: Yes.

Dealing with the tessitura

The tessitura of this aria is tricky. I find it a good practice to try parts of it half step higher than written. Sometimes that half step allows you to feel things differently and helps with intonation when returning to the original key. You can choose to try the entire piece up the half step or just four to eight measures at a time. Another practice tip is to go pitch to pitch, without regard to rhythm, and sing a portamento between each note. This helps you feel how to carry the sound when the top informs the bottom, and the bottom informs the top. Again, slow and steady is a good idea, with four to eight measures at a time.

Final "d'amore" (exercise from Part 1)

The final cadenza is traditionally not what is in the piano/vocal score. Most tenors know immediately what to sing and where to find it as it is such an well-established cadenza. At the end of the cadenza the pitches are F_4 (in the passaggio), with a *fermata* down a fifth to $B♭_3$. The word is *amor.* If you put your /a/ in a more closed space by slightly rounding the vowel at the beginning of this often-difficult pitch, you will have more control as well as more facility to crescendo from a true *pianissimo* to the *portamento* down. The exercises from Part 1 will help with this as well (arpeggio and messa di voce)

Verdi, *La traviata,* "Deh, miei bollenti spiriti"

Story

The original source of this beautiful story is the play by Alexandre Dumas *fils*, author of *La Dame aux camélias.* I encourage you to read the play even before you dive into the music. It will inform so much of what you will choose, especially if you then compare it to the libretto of Francesco Maria Piave. What is the same as the original story? What is different? Why? These are fun things to find in a variety of google searches and in the library!

After the end of Act I and the iconic aria "Sempre libera," we are left wondering what Violetta and Alfredo choose to do. It is summed up briefly in the opening of Act 2, "Lunge da lei… De' miei bollenti spiriti." (Note: In the original play, there is an act between Acts 1 and 2 that is not included in the opera.) The translation of the recitative is essential to your understanding of the story. First section: *Away from her, there is no delight for me. Three moons (month) have flown by since my Violetta left (for me!) duty, honor/love*[3]*, and the excitement of the parties, to which she'd become accustomed, as each person paid homage to her beauty.* Second section: *And now she's content in this pleasant place, having forgotten it all...for me.* Third section: *Here next to her, my senses are reborn. And by the breath of love I'm regenerated, lost in the joy with her, and the past is completely forgotten.* In the aria, he declares that since she has promised her fidelity to him, he's incredibly happy, living as if he's in heaven.

Most tenors, in audition or recital, limit the aria to recit and aria, not continuing on with the cabaletta, "Oh mio rimorso! Oh infamia!" However, before accepting an offer to sing the role, make sure you review this carefully and ask if it will be included or cut, as it is quite difficult to sing. Indeed, many professionals in the operatic world would insist that you *only* attempt aria if you can sing the cabaletta. The same is true for roles such as Des Grieux in Massent's *Manon*: most young singers can handle his first aria (The Dream), but the Saint Sulpice scene and the aria "Ah, fuyez" require a much larger, more dramatic voice.

Text

Always begin by speaking the text as a story or monologue, with meaning and as close to native inflection as possible. Once you are truly comfortable with the text, speak it gently in rhythm. You can use a metronome with the speaking part to keep your tempo steady. Once you have achieved that, sing the text in rhythm on one pitch (no metronome when you sing). Eventually choose pitches that are in the same tessitura as the phrase so that you are closer in the ballpark of where you need to be to sing the aria. I suggest spending a lot of time on the shaping of this text vis-a-vis the comments above and below.

Recitative shape

Alfredo runs onstage during the string *allegro vivace* introduction to the recitative. We sense the music as happy, and knowing the story, expect that he is anxious to be with Violetta again after his morning hunt. In the first section of the recitative, the listener finds out a bit of what has happened in the time between the end of Act 1 and the current scene. The accompaniment offers only one sustained chord underneath the text. Section two offers a change both musically and dramatically. It is achieved more easily by using the text *di sua bellezza* as the pivot point. No longer stating the facts, he leads us to Violetta's happiness in the *andante,* supported by eighth notes in the orchestra. The third section relaxes into an *adagio.* The orchestra shepherds the singer through the harmonic changes as Alfredo speaks of his personal changes, being reborn, regenerated, and reconciled with the past. Where to breathe in those last measures of the recitative? That is a very individual choice. I encourage listening to ten recordings (see Part 2 of this book) to see

[3] Some editions use the word *onori*, while others substitute *amori*

what the various options are. Try them all out. What feels best for you? What sounds best in your voice. What you choose as a singer at age 25 is possibly different than what you'll sing at 35. The biggest criteria are how it sounds in your voice and what technical capabilities you have right now.

Aria tempo

The aria proper is one of only a few musical moments in the entire score that does not have a metronome mark per the original manuscript, so, the indication of ♩ = 60 is editorial. The orchestra sounds a bit restless, especially when juxtaposed with the serenity at the end of the recitative and over the vocal line of the aria. Consider the speed of the sixteenth notes in the violin and viola *pizzicati* when setting your tempo. We want it to feel restless—not ruthless!

Articulation and dynamics

One of the keys to musical success in this aria is continuing the energy and the sound on the dotted notes, which helps with legato and line. When the notes indicate a staccato or portato, you need to determine the best way to accomplish this with your technique and in consultation with your teacher; it is not an opportunity simply to disconnect and offer a pogo stick approach, but rather a different articulation to the text, or the use of *détachée,* which is usually attributed to breath support. When singing *io vivo quasi in ciel*, notice the crescendo over two measures before the word *vivo,* arriving at a *forte,* with a quick one measure decrescendo to the *triple-piano* (*ppp* or *pianississimo*) on the word *quasi,* as if in heaven. The next time *vivo* is sung it is indicated as *fortissimo.* Perhaps these dynamics are representative of Alfredo's passion and temperament. In general, make sure you have core to your sound in the sixteenth notes, even if they are indicated to be staccato.

Cadenza

Having listened to ten recordings, you have likely heard several cadenzas as well, or at least ten different interpretations of the cadenza offered in most piano/vocal scores. Make sure your intonation is impeccable. Using the various daily tools in Part 1, you will have the tools for success when you break down this cadenza. For example, the first few pitches are the arpeggio for B♭ major with the added sevenths. The first pitch is the leading tone to the B♭ scale. What follows is the 1-3-5 in the arpeggio. Skip the G for a moment and you have the lowered seventh in the B♭ arpeggio. Practice that sequence so that it is a stabilizing factor in the beginning of your cadenza and then go back to look at the F-G-A♭ as the first three pitches of the F-minor scale. Once secure in both exercises, combine them to sing the first six notes of the cadenza.

Next, follow the outline of the same B♭-major arpeggio from the lowered seventh down; A♭-F-D-B♭, which should be easy as you've been practicing both ascending and descending arpeggios in your daily practice. (And if not, you can add it in, beginning today. Arpeggios are everywhere!) Next, look at the three-note groupings following the A♭4: A♭-E-F, F-C♯-D, D-A-B♭. Work on the integrity of the intonation within those smaller groupings. At the same time, practice the last four notes before the sixteenth rest, B-D-C. When they feel comfortable and are consistently sung in tune (record yourself to double check), start stringing them together five notes at a time. The first one will be the easiest. However, it will be trickier when you begin on E as your ear is not used to starting on that pitch. Once you can start on any of the notes in that sequence with excellent intonation, add the ascending line to the A♭. You're nearly at the end! The final *io vivo quasi in ciel* is easier than the beginning of the cadenza. Begin on the fermata (G_4) with the /u/ sound. Play around with a *messa di voce* there so that you know your possibilities. To say the word *quasi* just add the /k/. I find it better to IPA the word /kua-zi/ than with a /w/ as the Italian alphabet does not have a W in it, and we often spread the subsequent vowel if we think of the word as /kwa-zi/. When you add the *in ciel* to the end, be sure to hold the E♭ for at least three beats; actually, I think it is a good exercise to hold it for as long as you can. When you have gone through all these practice steps, singing the entire cadenza will feel more like coming home at the end of the aria rather than something to be feared.

Puccini, *La bohème,* "Che gelida manina"

Story

So, once again, we turn to the original source, this time by Henri Murger. The collection that became the book *Scènes de la vie de bohème* began as individual stories published in a Parisian magazine. Before it became a book, it took a turn as a play titled *La Vie de Bohème.* The origin of this work is a wonderful rabbit hole to go down in your non-singing research, as you can find many fun facts and hypotheses about all the characters in the opera, such as the author himself as the inspiration for Rodolfo!

Set the scene

This is yet another iconic aria that sets the scene for romance. After all, in searching for Mimi's lost key when the candles have been extinguished, he finds her key, puts it in his pocket, and seeks her hand "by accident," which begins the aria when he sings *Che gelida manina, se la lasci riscaldar*, (paraphrased, what a frozen hand [you have], let me warm it up [for you]). He then shares who he is, much like happens on many first dates. And remember, he is a poet! He uses language in a way that is more thoughtful than most of his peers, such as when he sings *Per sogni e per chimere e per castelli in aria, l'anima ho milionaria* (For dreams and chimeras and for castles in the air, I have the soul of a millionaire). Let your Rodolfo love his language each time he speaks.

Where to start

Many singers and pianists start the aria two full measures before the singing begins, on the A♭ (which is often connected to the moment Rodolfo finds Mimi's hand). To me, this is a missed opportunity. I suggest starting seven measures earlier with the three eighth notes from the violin. It sets the scene, and especially in an audition, allows you to hear the acoustics of the room, the sound of the piano, and the style and ability of the pianist, all important information before you begin.

Recitative in the aria

While the entire piece is considered an aria, there are moments that function more as a recitative. Be sure you know where they are, which allows you to know where to be more expressive with the text, and when to let the melody soar. For example, for me the opening line functions as an accompanied recitative. It is important to use those several measures to prepare for the A♭4 and the higher tessitura of *Cercar che giova*? Whenever there are repeated notes that are lower in your range, it is likely a spot to think about as recitative such as *Aspetti signorina, Chi son*? *Che cosa faccio*?

Rhythm

As in many Puccini arias, the orchestra syncopation on the upbeats keeps the momentum going without being aggressive or boisterous. It is important to note that the rhythm of the orchestra shifts away from the syncopation at the *andante lento*, for the text *In povertà mia lieta*. These rhythmic shifts can be looked at as emotional shifts as well. Listen to how the music and orchestral colors change to match or introduce the change of character in the aria. We are at the heart of who he is as a man and poet. And then the lovely triplets come in creating even more energy and excitement *Talor dal mio forziere* even as the dynamic is *piano* (remember that Puccini's *piano* is often played by dozens of strings!).

Articulation and Tempo

Puccini has written what he wants, so adherence to dynamics and articulation is essential. For example, the notes of *e qui la luna* have a tenuto mark over them to provide emphasis. By adding the *rallentando,* the voice is allowed to soar to the top of the phrase before adhering to the *affrettando* on the second syllable of *l'abbiamo* only to return to a *poco ritardando* on syllables two and three of *vicina*. And how unbelievably charming is the next line, *Aspetti signorina*, with the tenuto marks and the double /t/ asking Mimi to wait and hear more of his story. I encourage singers to mark the tempo indications by highlighting in yellow or marking in red. This way, the visual aid helps the singer know what happens when, and what the composer is asking. I also suggest marking the dynamics in red pencil. It is important to memorize all these markings when committing a musical selection to memory. If you only memorize the pitches, rhythms, and words, you are missing at least half of the story.

As previously noted, (page 76) the young Maestro Arturo Toscanini conducted the world premiere in 1896. One would assume that he knew just what Puccini wanted from the score. I absolutely adore the NBC Symphony Orchestra recording released by RCA from 1946, conducted 50 years later by Maestro Toscanini. It is (often) radically different from what we hear today, but I can't help thinking that Toscanini knew better than anyone else.

High pitches

Yes, this is a difficult aria. The climatic C_5 is high: it feels high and it sounds high to listeners. I would suggest practicing *la speranza*[4] when you are your freshest, after a good warm up. Know what you need to do for success. Practice the success repeatedly over time and then back up to *poichè, poichè v'ha preso stanza*, realizing the same success for your C_5. Don't leave your practice of that phrase for where it lies in the aria, as you are likely to be fatigued by this point. Once your body knows how to sing it well and successfully, then add it to the aria by backing up four to eight measures at a time until you are finally at the top of the aria.

Carrying and Binding (aka Portamento and Legato)

Please review the general comments and practice tips from earlier in this chapter. While the musical style is different the concepts are the same.

---

[4] The climactic high-C falls on the /ɛ/ in first syllable of *speranza,* rather than the stressed, second syllable, /a/, as might be expected. Puccini almost certainly did not understand voice acoustics, but he realized his tenors sounded better when singing closed vowels, such as /e ɛ æ u o ɔ/ for their highest pitches. We now, of course, understand this preference to be based on the resonance intersections of the vowel with the pitch being sung.

Key

The key of this aria is D♭ major—or is it? Actually, the original autograph presented the aria in the key of C major. While I'm not sure of all the details that surrounded this decision to make a change, Puccini nonetheless chose to shift the key up a half step to D♭. His publisher (Ricordi) was unhappy about this, and singers of the time often would transpose it back down. In the published score, Puccini won out and the key is and always has been D♭, which is the current expectation. However, there have been situations and circumstances when a tenor has chosen the lower key for performance (even in some major opera houses). For young singers, I would insist on the key of D♭. If you choose to experiment with C major, realize that because it becomes a tad easier to sing, you must careful not to add extra vocal weight, which could get you into trouble later in the aria. You also could find yourself summarily dismissed from further consideration because you offered a non-standard, some would say easier, key. When you are hired for your first Rodolfo, the opera company is likely expecting you to sing the aria in D♭ (negotiation might be possible).

Additional information

For the savvy pianist, there are some wonderful orchestral colors that didn't make it into the piano/vocal score. It's worth checking out the orchestra score and adding things that you hear in recordings to support the color of the aria.

Pesky Passages

Mozart, *Così fan tutte,* "Un' aura amorosa"

Let's face it, almost all the Mozart arias are difficult and have a high tessitura, so, what is to be said about this beautiful aria also holds true for most of his other tenor arias. The range and tessitura are challenging, so you must be certain of where you are going musically and vocally, and how you will get there. One of the biggest problems in this (and other tenor Mozart arias) is intonation. Fatigued by the last page and a half, it is hard to keep in the center of the pitch and to keep everything in tune. I would suggest singing your most difficult passages as well as the return of *Un' aura amorosa* on a vowel both half step lower and half step higher. You need to know the territory. One of the three keys will feel the best for you, and you can use that as the map for success with intonation. Also, practice in four measure groupings. This way, you can stay fresh and keep your sound spinning, which will help with intonation.

Intonation issues occur most frequently with the half steps and whole steps (please refer to Part 1 for daily exercises to reinforce the accuracy of those intervals). Also, the arpeggios need focused attention, especially the D-major arpeggio at the end on *un dolce ristoro*, which starts out, after the A_3 anacrusis, on that pesky, repeated F♯$_4$. Like climbing up and down a ladder where you need to know by feeling just where to put your feet, you need to know how to get down safely (vocally) from the F♯$_4$ to the D_4, to the A_3, to the lower F♯$_3$ to the final D_3 on the phrase. But beware, the next phrase has you once again on that A_4. In practice, I would start with the high A, portamento down to the E_4 and then sing the A again, which will let you know just how you need to sing that E. In general, look to the top pitch of the phrase to inform how you will sing the first note of the phrase.

And the aria is slow, making it even more exposed. *Coraggio!*

Verdi, *Rigoletto,* "La donna è mobile"

Among the many challenges in this aria, there are three I'd like to point out. First is the tempo. With the time signature of 3/8, a choice must be made as to whether the aria is in one or three. I've worked with enough productions to know that both are an option. For the singer, it is crucial that you think about the duration of the phrase. For example, the phrase *La donna è mobile qual piuma al vento* is sung in four measures. It is very easy to think vertically and emphasize each beat; however, it's not particularly musical or good for your voice. Think of the first four measures as one measure of four, which will help you think of the length of the phrase and create a line for your music: a vocal GPS. The second four measures complete the sentence and allow you to have created a longer phrase.

The second issue is that too often many of the notes are clipped, resulting in a bumpy ride for the listener. Now, I know you do not approach this aria in the same manner as you would "Un aura amoroso," but there still must be line and legato in your approach. There is a section in Part 3.5 (Mezzo Examples) for "Smanie implacabili" that would be helpful to read. Applying it here, you would simply sing the phrases with the sixteenth notes as eighth notes, without the rests. See where your voice and line want to go, and then, erase the sound for the rests, which will prevent the clipped sound referenced above. Pavarotti is the perfect example for listening to this aria. He pays attention to all the articulation but is totally aware of his legato and line.

The third pesky part is the descending B-major scale that starts on the seventh tone. Be sure you have practiced your scales well (see Part 1) and that you know exactly where the 32nd notes are in your voice and sound. Too often they are either X notes (see Part 1.3, page 21) or not in the center of the pitch which makes for a sloppy end of the first verse and often an out of tune final note.

Mozart, *Don Giovanni,* "Il mio tesoro"

If you are ready to work on "Il mio tesoro," go directly to measures 42 through 48 because they usually are the most challenging part of the aria. In working on the clarity of the sixteenth notes, review Part 1.4, the section called Rhythms for Practice, which will help you begin to tackle this long phrase with accuracy. The second issue is breath control. Many singers take a breath after the E♭4 in measure 45. Know what you are capable of before you determine the tempo for the aria. Too many singers set a lovely *andante* tempo only to speed up here because they run out of breath. Some singers avoid this issue by adjusting the text underlay to take a quick breath before *asiugar.* The same applies to the pickup to measure 65 through measure 70, as well as measures 75 to 78. We can all hear when you rush (or when you've asked the pianist to rush) to make it easier for you. Practice these pesky parts first, so you know what is attainable when you start "from the beginning."

Part 3.7

Baritone Examples

During my coaching sessions, singers often present the same or similar difficulties, which might be related to pitch, rhythm, text, phrase direction, or interpretation. Fortunately, there are solid practice solutions for making corrections. Please refer to your piano/vocal score when reading this section.

Gounod, *Faust,* "O sainte médaille...Avant de quitter ces lieux"

Did you know that this beautiful aria was not included in the opera for its world premiere? It was added, in English, in 1864, for the starring baritone, conceived from a theme first presented during the overture. It was subsequently translated into French and has become an iconic baritone aria and one of the most familiar tunes from *Faust.* (I have heard that the scene was originally a duet where Marguerite gave Valentine the holy medallion but cannot confirm that.) Feel free to work on this aria for several years before presenting it in your audition package or in recital! It is difficult to master, and like a beautiful antique piece of furniture, needs time and care for it to turn out well and last over time.

Recit to Aria

Following the brass introduction, Valentine addresses the *sainte médaille* (a holy medallion with the image of a saint) that his sister has given him for protection during battle. The most common cut takes the three chords in measure eleven, sustains the top pitch, D, on beat three through the measure, before continuing three full measures before the Cavatina begins. (Some pianists include beats two through four of the fourth measure before the Cavatina, the three quarter-notes on D.) It's not a bad idea to do some research on the significance of holy medals in the Roman Catholic tradition, especially during the Sixteenth century (when the opera takes place) as well as the 1800s when Gounod was living.

Above the staff

The first two vocal lines of the Cavatina are misleading; the rest of the aria features a higher tessitura. If you focus too keenly on that part of your voice, you are likely not going to be successful three and five measures later when the $E\flat_4$, F_4, and G_4, need to be sung beautifully. In the first measure of the Cavatina, I would write the upcoming high G_4 into my score so I always could see the prompt and would begin the aria with that G in mind. Sometimes it is helpful simply to think (and pretend) that the vocal entrance is an octave higher than it actually is, which helps you get to the text *ma soeur* with a better frame of reference. This first section has a beautiful, memorable melody that needs line and legato. The second section lives consistently in a higher tessitura. I suggest working on this section early in your practice sessions so that you are fresh and can plan just what you need to do to sing it well. And remember that legato and line are needed in this section, too! In the recapitulation (or third section), don't get too comfortable on the first four measures. Use them well to rest up for the final stretch of the aria. Because of the high tessitura, this section also should be practiced when your voice is fresh. Lip and tongue trills can be helpful for coordinating your breath. Depending on where your voice is most comfortable, it can sometimes be a good idea to sing four measures half step higher. That often prepares you better for the high notes to come. As always, vowel work will do wonders for feeling where the musical line wants to go. You will need to give the pianist a strong vocal GPS to follow. Remember also that dynamics are your friend. Start the aria at *piano* so you have somewhere to go with your dynamics and color palette. Another good practice tip is to sing the text at performance tempo on one pitch only; this can help you focus on what the language needs to do to help support the vocal line. When practicing the sections with large skips, a good practice strategy is to sing a portamento down so to keep your sound focused throughout your range. For example, in the first two measures of the aria, you sing B♭3 and then C3 on the word *quitter.* A good practice portamento can help you align your sound and focus. After several *portamenti*, try the interval and think about the *portamento* but don't sing it. It can help you "carry" the sound evenly.

Accompaniment

It is important for both singer and pianist to note what is and is not in the piano/vocal score, which includes things that are not found in the orchestra score. Curiously, there also are notes and rests and tempo indications in the orchestra score that are not found in the piano/vocal score. Most notably, some oboe lines are missing that are crucial to the melodic shape of the orchestra and the A♭ played by the viola on beat four before the recapitulation. While it is not necessary to play, it is important to note that Valentine's melody is often doubled in the orchestra, therefore correct rhythm is key. If I were you, I would be sure to do my homework and create a piano reduction that included everything essential as it will ultimately support what you want to bring to the aria.

Tempo

It always is important to know how to change a tempo on your first measure to ensure the musical choices truly are yours. Marking metronome indications is a great way to help the pianist take your tempo; otherwise, they are likely to play a tempo from their last singer or that they have played most frequently. The *poco andante* in many piano/vocal scores is not in the orchestra score. Be sure you know your tempo so that you can change it on the first two quarter notes you sing. The same holds true for the tempo change to the *un poco più animato* section with dotted eighth/sixteenth notes. Take charge of your tempo, whether it is charging forward or harnessing a runaway tempo, and remember that the recapitulation should be the same tempo as the opening of the Cavatina.

Strauss, *Ariadne auf Naxos,* "Lieben, Hassen"

Harlekin (sometimes called Harlequin) and his *commedia dell' arte* troupe are pushed into performing concurrently with an *opera seria* as the entertainment for the evening. If they don't perform, they don't get paid, and the opera singers already have taken the stage to fully realize their production. So, there are frequent interjections by the *commedia dell' arte* troupe amid the soaring phrases of the *opera seria*. During his turn, Harlekin attempts to cheer up Ariadne—a very sad, lamenting woman—encouraging her to give life a second chance. Also, I believe it is always good to have a short aria in your package. At roughly 90 seconds to two minutes, this aria packs a punch, showing the listener your sound, your musicianship and musicality, and your dramatic ability. If done well, it will be remembered and leave the listener wanting more.

Text

Lieben, Hassen, Hoffen, Zagen are the words that open the aria: Love, Hate, Hope, Fear. They are a study in text painting. What color is *Hassen*, what sentiment is *Hoffen*? These are choices that you must make, taking into mind the translation as well as the dynamics and articulation that Strauss has given you.

- *Lieben* (to love) is indicated with *piano.* It is also a dotted rhythm, much like you would use in speech
- *Hassen* (to hate) is indicated with two accents and equal eighth notes
- *Hoffen* (to hope) has no dynamic marking on the vocal line, but the orchestra (and piano/vocal) score has *piano.* The rhythm is even eighth notes
- *Zagen* (to fear) is indicated with *pianissimo* and, again, a dotted rhythm

These words deserve a good deal of work. Speak the text with a variety of emotions that convey their meaning, and then speak the text in rhythm, again with a variety of emotions. Concurrently, you can sing the pitches and rhythms (one at a time) multiple times to find the right vocal colors, shapes and meaning to the words. I would have one day be set aside for *Lieben*, the next day would be *Hassen*, and so forth. Playing with the words will allow you to be comfortable with the text, its feeling in your mouth, and its emotional context. When I hear this aria in an audition, I am keenly aware of the depth of your work by how you sing these first two measures. Make them count!

Dynamics and rhythms

The buoyant and playful rhythms in this aria partner with Harlekin's objective of cheering up the woeful Ariadne. It must always have legato and line; however, within that context you have some lovely texture.

The aria starts with sixteenth notes pizzicati, which continue throughout. Let this help you with your playfulness and buoyancy. Syncopations are everywhere, so have fun. If all the syncopations were removed, the character of the aria would be lost. Additionally, for the text *und so mußt du mir nicht sein*, the rhythm of the orchestra/piano are different. Enjoy that moment. Be sure you've worked the rhythm for accuracy, but then, again, have fun. You are Harlekin! This also happens earlier (and more subtly) in the text *einmal um das andre Mal.*

Arpeggios and range

After the important work of the first two measures, range and arpeggios must be considered. While the first two measures are middle range, measure three takes you immediately to the F_4 by way of an arpeggio. I would suggest significant arpeggio practice (see Part 1) on the pitch F_3. After that is easy, sing the F_4 on *Lust* with a *portamento* to the A_3 of the first measure, which will help inform how to begin that phrase vocally. Writing in the F_4 in your score with your opening breath mark can remind you of where you will be going very soon!

Toward the end of the aria, on the text *Mußt dich aus dem Dunkel heben wär es auch um neue Qual! Leben mußt du*, you must successfully sing from C_3 to F_4. I would suggest the scale exercise in Part 1 of the daily tools to help you with this. Keep the C_3 measure buoyant with the syncopation and the sixteenth notes as you begin your journey to the F_4. It is also *pianissimo* which is good! It allows you to shape the line with text and articulation until you get to *auch um neue Qual*! where the crescendo allows you to grow your sound and volume. With a breath after *Qual* you're right in line for your F_4—provided you didn't drop everything during the breath! And if that F is in the sweet spot, enjoy the moment with a lingering *espressivo* that then leads us to the end of the phrase.

Rossini, *Il barbieri di Siviglia,* "Largo al factotum"

This is a beast of an aria and I applaud any baritone who makes any attempt! But there are many singers who successfully sing the role, and I'm sure they have put in very hard work: the various skills required for this aria are far from easily acquired. It is a light-hearted, confident, happy four-minute sing—to himself! It is also an aria open to many different interpretations. Be sure to listen to ten different recordings (preferably before beginning the aria) so you have an idea of what is possible and aligns with your style, taste, and ability. I would also suggest a shorter introduction when singing this in an audition. The audition clock starts when you walk into the room. Seven measures before *Largo* is sufficient.

Dynamics, tempo, and articulation

Beginning *allegro vivace* we all know we're in for a ride! That pace is kept throughout most of the aria. The *a piacere* sections allow a moment of respite for the listener as well as the singer. Please use that time wisely for artistic choice as well as rest. The aria concludes with a *stringendo* that makes for an exciting close. Make sure you practice it regularly and well so that, even if fatigued, you know how to sing it.

The aria also begins *piano.* The first forte is in the third measure of singing on the E_4 *Largo*. The dynamics are there to help you. This is not an aria for full throttle singing all the time. Let the dynamics of the orchestra inform what you do as well. I suggest marking your dynamics in red pencil so that you have a visual reminder of **what** changes and **when**, each time you practice. The dynamic contours of the *a piacere/col canto* before rehearsal number 35 in the Ricordi score (the repetitions of his name Figaro) can help as a place to rest and recombobulate. We'll follow your contours and be ready for your *Ahimè* and the frenzy you talk about!

Articulations can be your friend; it is the composer's way of letting you know what his intent is regarding how the aria is sung and perceived. We start with *staccato* (please remember that your line always remains intact—*staccato* doesn't mean chopped). If done well this allows for a lovely texture change to *legato* several measures later with the text *che bel piacere*.

Rhythm

Please pay close attention to your rhythms, working on them with neutral syllables to reinforce the needed accuracy. I would suggest setting a metronome at a reasonable speed and without singing, simply work on the rhythms. You'll feel very confident for the first few pages, I suspect. But after Rehearsal 33 in the Ricordi score, beware of beats one, two, and three; too many singers sing the rhythm as quarter/eighth rather than eighth/eighth/eighth rest. That is the same for that entire section as well as the section between rehearsal numbers 34 and 35.

Pitches

Again, on a neutral syllable slowly work on the pitches. Choose eight measures at a time and really sing in the middle of the pitch. Too often I hear what I refer to as X notes (see Part 1.3, page 21) in the speed and heat of the moment, which creates a bumpy ride for the listener and is not particularly helpful for your voice. Beware of the pattern first presented in measures five and six after the singing begins, which needs to be clean—the only pitches are D and G. A similar arpeggiated phrase occurs several measures later the next set of *la ran la la* repetitions: If you are sloppy here, it is likely you will be sloppy everywhere.

The next super tricky spot is after Rehearsal 33 on the text *La la ran la* where the middle note of each set of three often is overlooked. Sing the outline once or twice: G, A♭, A♮ , B♭, B♮ , C, D, E♭—all half steps except for the C to D sequence. Use the exercises in Part 1 that emphasize the middle of the three notes so that you are aware of when the middle note is a half step and when it is a whole step. Many of us know the aria well enough to hear when you've put in the work.

One place that is particularly tricky for the tessitura is shortly after Rehearsal 35 when there are several repetitions of F_4 and E_4 on the text *uno alla volta*. Let the vowels be like vegetables for your voice and help you with that tricky spot. The repeated E_4 before this requires stamina and skill. This is a phrase to work early on with your teacher so that you get on the right track from the beginning.

The next section needs to be used as a resting place. Yes, you must sing, but you must know how to use the rests and lowered tessitura of the section to your benefit.

The final stretch requires work like what you did at Rehearsal 33—you need to learn the outline, of course, but the middle pitch/note is the linchpin for accuracy. Again, using the exercises in Part 1 will be incredibly helpful; otherwise, it just sounds like you're shaking your sound. The recordings you have listened to will help you make the choice for how to end the piece. For example, do you want to omit two measures before the final *della città*, or hold the final C_4 until the end of the eighth notes, or sing *La la la* with the orchestra for the last few measures before the final chords. There are lots of choices for you to make. The only rule that I think should be hard and fast is this: Only choose to perform what you can do well and securely. As your technique develops you will be able to incorporate more into your interpretation.

Text

This aria is a mouthful! Using a metronome (and only eight measures at a time) begin in rhythm with a setting of ♩. = 60, gradually working your way up to ♩. = 160. Yes, it is super fast, but practicing at this speed will make a performance tempo of 136 or so seem less intimidating. This can be tedious work, but it gets your mouth used to the text in a way that will serve you well going forward. If you are too bumpy at the slow tempo, you will likely lose that bumpiness when faster. I call it going from the trot to the gallop (see Part 2.1, page 50)

There is an exercise I like to give singers who sing this aria that I learned from my friend and Italian teacher, Robert (Bob) Cowart, who would take the phrase *tutti mi chiedono, tutti mi vogliono, donne, ragazzi, vecchi, e fanciulle* and speak each pitch in rhythm without rests except for the eighth rest after *ragazzi*. He would have the singer start slowly and speed up, as described in the previous paragraph.

Another quick mention in honor of my friend, Bob, is to pay attention to the open and closed vowels in this aria. We should always pay attention to this, but my score is particularly marked with the open and closed vowels that Bob insisted I put in my score as a young coach in New York City. One word of special interest is *risorsa:* Be sure that the S is pronounced /s/ rather than /z/.

Who are you?

Figaro is the quintessential jack of all trades, as we learn during the aria and opera. Everyone wants a piece of him. You can't simply *act* Figaro, you need to *become* Figaro. A deep dive in the activities in Part 2 of this book will be helpful, and also, look at the dramatic resources in the Appendix. If you must think too much about who you are, you will lose the ability to successfully sing and be a convincing character. Be sure to read the original Beaumarchais trilogy to understand Figaro and his trajectory.

Pesky Passages

Mozart, *Le nozze di Figaro,* "Hai già vinta la causa"

There are a few pesky places in this aria from Act 3 as well as an interesting diversion that one can take. First, it is important to know that the Count does not start the recitative with his own words. He overhears a conversation between Figaro and Susanna:

> *Taci: senza avvocato hai già vinta la causa. Cos'è nato*? Susanna: "Be quiet; without a lawyer, you have already won the cause/lawsuit." Figaro: "What's happened?"

The aria is his reaction to what he's heard. The C-major chord is simply a pitch giver when the aria is excerpted and should be played without regard to tempo of the measure. In an audition or concert, it can serve, as the mnemonic device to process what the Count is overhearing.

The recitative must convey how the Count is figuring out what is happening. First, he repeats to himself what he just overheard between Figaro and Susanna. The next change, at the *presto*, reflects his anger and desire for punishment. The *andante* shifts his thoughts as the text reflects with the word *Ma*, which in Italian is the conjunction "but," and changes the direction of thought. And then we talk about Antonio, which is a section of more secco type recitative: *E poi v'è Antonio che all'incognito Figaro ricusa di dare una nipote in matrimonio*. That is a long sentence and needs much work to make it sound like a native Italian.

Pesky triplets are found in the *allegro assai*, followed by the high F♯4. If you have not kept that climactic note in your sights since the beginning of the aria, chances are that you will not be successful in its execution. And difficult triplets are found several measures before that F♯4, making it even more taxing. As indicated in the previous discussion of "Largo al factotum," find the outline, B D G B E G C♯, and sing it a few times. But then, go to work on the middle note (see "Largo al factotum" and Part 1.3 of this book, *Working on Meter, Tempo, Rhythm, and Clarity*).

Now, for the interesting diversion. When I was in graduate school at the University of Illinois, I was introduced to the Oxford University Press publication of *W.A. Mozart LE NOZZE DI FIGARO, Eight Variant Versions,* by Alan Tyson. Two of the offerings are different versions of the final fast section, both with higher pitches than the edition more commonly used. I also understand that it is in the 2009 Bärenreiter piano/vocal score in the appendix. For baritones with high pitches, this is an exciting and fun diversion. Enjoy!

Verdi, *La traviata,* "Di provenza"

There is much to work on in this aria, but the hardest aspects are technical, so please visit them with your teacher before jumping into the learning process. The one thing I'd like to address is the legato line and the grace notes, which too often sound rather like a hiccup. I would encourage you brave baritones to sing the line beautifully legato *without* the grace notes for a few weeks. At the same time, you'll want to practice *only* the grace notes, such as the E_4 to D_4 in a variety of rhythms and articulations. This way you really know where they belong when you integrate the two. And it might not be a bad idea to work on the final cadenza first, three to four notes at a time so that you can work them into your voice in a healthy manner. *In bocca al lupo*.

Korngold, *Die tote Stadt,* "Tanzlied des Pierrot"

The *messa di voce* daily exercise in Part 1.2 will work wonders for this aria, which takes some bravery to sing because it is so exposed. Practice the exercise on the C_4 and $D\flat_4$ so you know what you can accomplish on those pitches with dynamics and color. When approached from below, make sure that you have prepared for the higher pitch. In fact, I think the exercise would benefit any note in this aria where the singer is encouraged to linger. What is possible for you to do? What is not? You need to know. You need to know for sure.

In some of the longer lines that require great breath support, I would encourage lip trills or tongue trills as a start or even at the beginning of practice when you know it well. It helps you think long and sustained. After that, go to various vowels and sing the lines with beautiful, focused, supported sound.

Part 3.7

Bass-Baritone and Bass Examples

During my coaching sessions, singers often present the same or similar difficulties, which might be related to pitch, rhythm, text, phrase direction, or interpretation. Fortunately, there are solid practice solutions for making corrections. Please refer to your piano/vocal score when reading this section.

Mozart, *Die Zauberflöte,* "In diesen heil'gen Hallen"

Mozart's interest in the Masonic Order is woven into the fabric of the story and music of this Singspiel. I know there are many different opinions about the significance of the that influence and that there also might be influence from the Enlightenment, religion, and philosophy. (This would be a fun google search to follow!) Archaic language, improper actions, and questionable ethics are also part of the opera. How these issues are presented ultimately is the choice of the production team and I would hope they would give this serious consideration when determining production values and storytelling.

In this second act aria, Pamina has pleaded with Sarastro to show clemency to her vengeful mother, the Queen of the Night. Sarastro sings this gentle aria about love, light, forgiveness, and the path to enlightenment within his holy halls, which are the elements that must be presented, rather than the discombobulated and confused underlying message of the opera, in this elegantly simple aria structured as a two-verse song.

Breath

In these long lines, it is important to get a secure and good breath before each phrase. Practice each phrase independently so you know exactly what kind of breath to take and how to take it. After that is secure, you can look at the amount of time you have to take the breath. A good practice strategy is to first discover the breath you need, taking all the time you need. When you know how that feels, take the same breath in half the time. When that becomes habituated, breathe in half the time again, and so forth. This way, you already will know the quality of the breath you need when you get to the sixteenth note rests. It is always good to practice this aria as well on a vowel, letting it become "vegetables for the voice."

Legato and the German language

Listening to the German greats of the past 100 years will dispel any myth about the German language and difficulty with legato. All the great German artists sang with a beautiful legato, and so must you. The exercise I recommend is in several steps; however, each step takes time and brainpower to achieve. First, you must be able to speak the text as a poem or story, making sure that you speak in sentences rather than syllables. Record this as you go so that you can assess immediately if you have achieved the goal of legato. Second, sing the text on one pitch. You choose the rhythm based on your spoken text. It is about text and legato. Again, record, listen, and assess. Third, sing the text on one pitch in the rhythm that Mozart set. As a fluent German speaker, we need to use the rhythm as a roadmap to what Mozart wanted to say. He could have chosen any rhythm. Why these? During the same practice period, sing these beautiful vocal lines on a vowel, choosing your best vowel first. How does the legato feel? After all these steps you are ready to integrate the words, pitches, and rhythms for beautiful legato phrases. Don't be over-ambitious. Try one phrase a day (one phrase, but two different verses).

Passing tones and appoggiature

Musically speaking, you need to know which pitches are passing tones and which are appoggiature. For example, in the first full measure of singing, the B_3 starts out as the fifth of the triad, which then on beat two becomes an appoggiatura. Carefully approach the F♯ arpeggio for good intonation to ensure the E_3 doesn't fall into either the lower part of the pitch, or simply become flat. In measure six, the G♯3 functions as an appoggiatura. Remember that this means to lean, so it is an important note in the phrase and not to be simply passed by. Measure twelve presents an E-major scale, which will be an important scale for you to practice as it starts on the 5th (pitch of the day in Part 1). This is a "two for the price of one" phrase as it repeats in the following measure. Since there are two verses it is really "four for the price of one." Also note that the G♯3 on the downbeat of measures thirteen and fifteen are both appoggiature. I suggest marking all the appoggiature so that you are constantly aware in your practice process.

Optional low pitches

Many people have come to expect the optional low pitches at the end of the second verse. If you are unfamiliar with this tradition, I suggest you review Part 2. 4 *The Research Behind What You Do* section of this book and listen to ten different recordings to hear what famous singers have done. What makes sense for you? If you have a beautiful, resonant, low E_2, it would be a wonderful option to consider. For the younger singer, only try this if you truly have the low sounds!

Mozart, *Le nozze di Figaro,* "Se vuol ballare"

Upon realizing that the Count intends to reverse his decision to abolish the *Droit du seigneur* and bed Susanna before she and Figaro have consummated their marriage, Figaro turns his anger into action and determines to take control of the situation himself in this Act 1 aria.

Who is Figaro?

As noted in Part 2 in this book, you should read the Beaumarchais play *La folle journée, ou Le marriage de Figaro* (it's fine in English translation!). Even better is to read the entire trilogy so that you get a more comprehensive picture of who Figaro is and who the Count is. Figaro is clever and witty. While the Rossini opera and the Mozart opera might take some liberties in the personalities of the characters, the play will give you a clearer through line of this amazing man. And remember, this is the same character who sings the "Largo al factotum" in Rossini's *Barbiere*.

Recitative

The first line, *Bravo, signor padrone*, is a sarcastic, biting remark as Figaro begins to understand the scheming of the Count. It is important to truly understand the text and the nuance in the language. From anger in the first line to deducing the Count's ultimate plan to take Susanna to London with him as his secret ambassador, Figaro makes it clear that he won't have it: He has spoken! So, while it only is fourteen measures long, it is an important recitative setting up the aria. Full of color, let your language choices in English reflect the deeper meaning of the Italian text. There are examples in Part 2. 1 *Working with language* that will help you bring this important page of music to life. Please be careful that you don't stress or elongate the final syllables of any of the sentences (except for the word *sarà). Mamma mia dice. Mamma mia padrone. Mamma mia mistero.* We all usually say *Mamma mia* correctly. So, use this as a prompt for your final syllables in the recitative.

Meter and tempo

The *allegretto* marking at the beginning of the aria and the 3/4 meter sets up the dance and the tone with the text "If you want to dance, little Count, I'll play the guitar for you." Figaro will control the situation. Note how you will sing the beginning repeated pitches of *Se vuol ballare*—paying attention to that lovely Italian double L in *ballare* and the double R in *chitarrino*) in a slightly different fashion than the line that is demanded with the descending scale starting in measure 23. Remembering *Mamma mia* is also good here for the two quarter notes on beats one and two. Note that beat three is a rest.

In the *presto* section, I suggest setting the metronome at a very slow speed for text work, in rhythm, four measures at a time, increasing the tempo by one or two notches after every successful attempt. You will need to be able to speak the text in rhythm much faster than you will need to sing it. This way, it can become muscle memory and you won't have to worry about the text so much. Only increase the tempo when you have achieved mastery, however. And your language should always be legato. This exercise can be done *sotto voce* or gently so as not to stress your voice, but it is still better to do this in three-to-five-minute chunks with a different practice activity in between (it takes a lot of mental focus). If you are too bumpy at the slow tempo, you will likely lose that bumpiness when faster. I call it going from the trot to the gallop (see Part 2.1, page 50).

High F_4

Never forget that you have the high F_4 to sing when you start from the F_3 at the beginning of the aria. A good strategy for this is to sing the F_4 with a *portamento* down to the F_3 and begin the aria that way. Letting it become your habit will ensure that you approach the first note correctly going forward. And then, there is the /i/ vowel. Find the F_4 first with your best vowel. From there let the /i/ start to creep in until you know just how you need to modify the vowel for the best sound. If it were me, I'd prefer to get a review about my great sound and adequate diction rather than perfect diction and compromised sound, but the ideal is to have both terrific sound and clear diction. It is a lifelong goal, especially on this tricky F_4 and the word *sì.* Using the strategy above, sing the F_4 with a *portamento* down to the G_3 and sing *le suonerò, sì* from that starting point. What you need to avoid is singing the F_4 in context and singing it tight and out of tune, otherwise that will become your habit.

Puccini, *La bohème,* "Vecchia zimarra senti"

Colline, the philosopher, decides to sell his coat to help pay for a doctor, medicine, or some other small comfort for Mimi in her dying moments. For the other friends, this decision might not warrant an aria, but for a philosopher, the need to consider the situation makes this (under) two-minute aria touching and moving. Somehow, Colline also knows that this is the end of life as they know it—the end of their bohemian lifestyle.

Legato and line

This aria is a study in line and legato and the phrases shift between reasonable and very long duration. Practice the phrases on a vowel, with perfect legato binding the notes together and with a vocal GPS that matches Puccini's phrasing. Work on one phrase at a time, taking the time you need to feel the shape of the phrase. For example, sing *io resto al pian, tu ascendere il sacro monte or devi* by itself, (both on a vowel and with the text) getting an appropriate breath before you start. If you always begin that phrase with a short, catch breath, you will concretize a compromised phrase and sound until it becomes a bad habit. Also note that Puccini's intent is to sing measure three with no extra breath. The energy must be maintained, so this exercise is especially important. Look at what else the composer has written in terms of long phrases that need legato and line, such as *ai non curvasti il logoro dorso ai ricchi ed ai potenti*; you will hear singers who break the phrase for a breath between the words *curvasti* and *il*, but you also will find singers who have figured out how to sing the phrase in one breath! Puccini also has written in a *portamento* on the words *come in* (between the B_3 and the $F\sharp_3$). Be sure you practice that independently so that you know just how you want to musically express that *portamento.* Little, light and late is always a good suggestion.

The space between the notes in the accompaniment, whether piano or full orchestra, necessitate a tremendous legato and line in this aria. You might feel a bit alone at times, but you still must keep your sound spinning. Lip trills and tongue trills can help with this as well.

Tempo

Fact: Puccini indicated the tempo as *allegretto moderato e triste.*
Fact: Puccini indicated a metronome mark, the ♩ = 63.
Fact: Most people sing it significantly slower.

As previously noted, (page 76 and 93) the young Maestro Arturo Toscanini conducted the world premiere in 1896. One would assume that he knew just what Puccini wanted from the score. I absolutely adore the NBC Symphony Orchestra recording released by RCA from 1946, conducted 50 years later by Maestro Toscanini. It is (often) radically different from what we hear today. Such is the case of this aria, which is pretty much at the tempo Puccini indicated. This recording is a vital piece of history for an iconic aria and opera, so be sure to listen to it. But also remember that taste and traditions often shift over time. Nonetheless, I would warn against making this sound like a funeral dirge.

You also need to know when to keep *a tempo,* when to slow down, and when to return to tempo. The two-page piano/vocal score has the following indications: *poco ritardando, poco rallentando, rallentando, molto ritardando.* Each one has a different feel, meaning and significance. Know which is which and what you intend to do.

You need to know exactly when the music is *a tempo* and when there is a change. I suggest that when you are comfortable and accurate with the text, you speak it in rhythm and tempo, but take it one step further. Make the *a tempo* quite brisk and the changes (which all slow the tempo down) very slow. This way, you know precisely where the changes occur with the text. Please don't rely on the pianist to lead you through these changes. The aria will then have the stamp of the pianist's interpretation rather than yours. And while it might be a very good interpretation, you, as the singer, need to take charge. A particular place to note is the return to *a tempo* on the text *filosofi e poeti.*

Drama and story telling
So, you are singing to a coat—an inanimate object, like Manon's little table—but it always is about more than the object. It is about the feelings. It is about its history. It is about the person. Practice singing to a photo, to a furry family member, to a person. This will help personify the object and leave you with a color palette of substance and depth.

Tessitura and range
I've been told by several singers that the tessitura of this aria can be difficult. I would suggest lip and tongue trills in the key that it's written. I would also suggest half step lower as well as half step higher. Help yourself make this an easier sing. At the very least, allow the half-step higher key to inform how you want to approach the key of C♯ minor.

The E♭4 on the word *passar* is marked *piano* and is preceded by the E3 on the /i/ vowel. While there is a breath there, it is crucial that you keep everything on track as you approach the higher pitch. Just as you don't turn off the car at each stop sign, you don't disengage your body, breath, or brain at every rest. A good practice technique is to go from the higher note to the lower note with a big *portamento* and back. Once that is comfortable, switch it. Start from the low note and *portamento* to the high note. There is a breath there, so when applying your practice to that section sing only two measures at first, the measures of ricchi *ed ai potenti. Passar*. One of the failings in singing this area is allowing the sound and energy to dissolve as you descend the scale. Sometimes it helps to think about ascending as the vocal line descends to keep the energy intact. The other issue is to have the vowel ready rather than the consonant. If you are preparing for the /p/ you are likely not thinking of the /a/. Sing a sustained /a/ and then add /p/ back to the mix, being careful not to double the /p/. Practice this from C4 to F4, which will help make the whole line easier.

The words *ti dico* can be tricky if you are unsure of the vowel you need. Play around with a variety of vowels only on *ti dico* to see what feels best and sounds best. Once you know for sure, migrate that /i/ vowel into that space.

Pesky Passages

Rossini, *Il barbieri di Siviglia*, "La calunnia"
After it is discovered that the Count is vying for the attention of Rosina, Don Bartolo's ward (and intended wife), Don Basilio has the idea to run the Count out of town by starting a rumor, a slanderous rumor, a *calunnia* so that the people of Seville will insist that he leave. This aria tells us how he can make it happen.

When I asked a young singer what *La calunnia* meant, he said, "A calumny." I asked him what that meant. He didn't know. So, word to the wise, be sure to translate all the words, even the English words in your translation if you don't know their meaning. Calumny means slander, lying to harm someone's reputation, malicious intent.

The original key (and the key in the Ricordi score) is D major. However, Ricordi kindly includes the aria in the key of C major in the Appendix. Which key to use? For a bass or bass/baritone to sustain the rising tessitura, C major usually fits the voice better (orchestra parts are readily available in this key.)

The rising half steps from *alla fin trabocca* through the section *come un colpo di cannone* can make it difficult for consistency and stamina. I suggest practicing this first without all the commotion that the aria demands. Make sure you can sing those notes as they creep up the scale before you add the articulation and comedy to it Otherwise you just might end up yelling or pushing yourself sharp. It is fun. Learn where it lies in your body before adding all the fun things to your sound. You can begin the fun things in your language work!

There are many text opportunities for word painting and onomatopoeia, such as *gentile, sottile, dolcemente, sussurrar. Sibilando scorrendo ronzando,* just to name a few in the first few sentences! When you have your exact translation (see Appendix) you can see for yourself all the possibilities of coloring the words and your sound.

A word to the wise, be careful of the two note phrases on *sotto il pubblico flagella per gran sorte va a crepar.* If they are tight, you will find them difficult, fatiguing, and potentially harmful. A fun way to sing this is to bounce your knees on each quarter note. It is nearly impossible to tighten muscles when you are bouncing and in motion.

The dynamic scope of the piece goes from *pianissimo* to *fortissimo.* It is important to consider this when working out dynamics. You don't want to get too loud too soon and have nowhere to grow.

And finally, be sure to catch your breath in the rests. You can even make it part of your dramatic presentation as this aria allows for comedy in the text, the body, and the sound!

Verdi, *Simon Boccanegra,* "Il lacerato spirito"

I caution young singers to sing with their own voice and not try to imitate the sounds of those amazing singers who have decades of age and experience under their belts, which directly applies to this aria. I know that it is often considered the bass/baritone national anthem, but please beware. You would not expect a two-year-old to run full steam the length of a football field and tackle a 250-pound lineman. Don't expect for your young bass/baritone self to be able to sing this either. Work a measure or two at a time, with your own voice, and for fun. Do this always with the supervision of your voice teacher.

Floyd, *Susannah,* "Hear me, O Lord"

This is an amazing aria with a cautionary tale that requires a wide vocal and dynamic range. Even more seasoned singers must be cognizant of the dynamic range, which begins loud, high, and powerful. Choose your vowel carefully. We need to understand you, but you need to understand your voice. Go first with your best vowel and then shape-shift to the vowel in the word in the text. (And remember, if you get the role, you will likely have to sing this on your knees!) The energy required to sustain this tessitura and emotion requires short, sustained practice periods, much like training for a marathon. You'll eventually be able to sing the whole thing well, but wouldn't you prefer to learn it incrementally and well? If you lose your patience, sing it from start to finish once a month and no more until you have the technique and stamina for a full throttle presentation.

Mozart, *Don Giovanni,* "Madamina, il catalogo è questo"

As indicated in the early part of this section for the *presto* section of Mozart's "Se vuol ballare,"I suggest setting the metronome at a very slow speed for text work, in rhythm, increasing the tempo by one or two notches after every successful attempt. Many of these phrases are divided up easily over four beats, such as, *V'han fra queste contadine*. For the longer phrases, divide up in chunks that you can successfully tackle. Again, you will need to be able to speak the text in rhythm much faster than you will need to sing it. This way it becomes muscle memory, and you won't have to worry about the text so much. Only increase the tempo when you have achieved mastery, however. And your language should always be legato. Remember that this exercise can be done *sotto voce* or gently so as not to stress your voice.

Part 3.8

Song Literature

This section will be devoted to practice tools for selected song literature. These are by no means the only ways to practice, but they will give you an idea of what and how to practice. When coaching, issues arise that must be addressed. What is included here are things that consistently come up with singers that do have solid practice habits. Please refer to your music when reading this section.

There are a few initial strategies for understanding the song you are working on that will be included here for application to all the songs.

Text

In each song it is important to read through the text in the original language as well as the English translation, which you might have created with the Translation Template found in the Appendix. This should be done multiple times to become familiar with and at ease with the language and how the words feel in your mouth. Next, read the original work of the poet. Did the composer omit or add things? Is the original version an individual unit, or is it part of a set or cycle? If it is part of a group, did the composer leave anything out? If so, can you determine why it was omitted? For example, in Robert Schumann's *Frauenliebe und -Leben* two things are omitted, including the final stanza of the second song, "Er, der herrlichste von allen," and the ninth poem of the original set, "Traum der eignen Tage." When I first performed the song cycle, I found and read the ninth poem repeatedly, which informed how I played the postlude and gives more information about the intent of the cycle. You can read it yourself if you play or sing this beautiful cycle and come to your own conclusions.

In addition to reading and researching the text and the poems, it is important to read something about the poet. Do they write literally? Are they symbolists? It is key to understanding the meaning to know the poet and what informed their writing and writing style. It is also a good idea to add basic information about the poet in program notes to complement those of the composer.

Dividing the text into verses

Many songs are in binary or ternary form, but even if the song is through-composed, there are usually verses in which the melody, harmony, rhythm, and accompaniment indicate that something has changed. So, the first step is to break down the verses. It is best to do this on your music so that you see, each time you practice, where the different verses start. Once you have the verses divided, add three words per verse as descriptors such as: Verse 1, ominous, chilly, foreboding; Verse 2, questioning, confused, irritated; Verse 3, resigned, peaceful, clarity. This way, each time you arrive at the verse it is clear what your intention is. I would suggest working on each verse individually for the greatest comprehension and clarity before stringing them all together. For those of you tethered to the color wheel, you can add a color to each verse as well (buying markers so that you see the color each time you practice). Using the example above, I might choose ice-blue or gray for verse one, dark red for verse two, and sage green for verse three. These are all personal, so there is no right or wrong.

Accompaniment

Look at the accompaniment; what part does it tell in the story? Is it a partnership in color and meaning, as found in *Frauenliebe und -Leben?* Does it partner with the voice in word painting? Does it provide harmonic structure only? When you look at the accompaniment you will gain even more insight into the intent of the composer and the song.

Schubert, "Die Forelle" (1817)

This famous song is a lively example of Schubert's writing. The original text included four verses, with the fourth verse being the moral to the story. But Schubert chose not to include those words in his composition, which makes me think this simply is a song about a fish. You can add multiple layers into that as well.

Accompaniment

The accompaniment always informs the vocal line and often the meaning, so it is essential for the singer to pay attention to the composer's intent with the piano. In the accompaniment of "Die Forelle" I can see the little fish twisting around playfully in the water, as indicated by the grouping of sixteenth notes in the accompaniment. There is great playfulness on the subsequent eighth notes, with the first being accented. This beautifully sets up verses one and two, describing the trout and his happiness as well as his cunning not to be captured by the fisherman. Things change however, in the third verse; we lose the friendly sixteenth notes that have accompanied every measure thus far, and instead of flipping the notes upward we are first in a tight pattern of five sixteenth notes for four measures and with a change to minor, pairing with the text "But finally the thief could wait no longer." This is followed by groups of three sixteenth notes, all the while focusing tighter and tighter to the text "the fisherman muddied the water." After three measures, we have repeated chords with rests leaving us in a bit of suspense as the narrator states: "And I could guess what was going to happen next." The following two measures word paint in the accompaniment, "so jerked the fisherman's rod" as do the next two measures, with their denser texture and repeated sixteenth notes, "the little fish struggled on it." With a quick return to major, one must decide why! The text states "and I, with boiling blood, saw the deceived one." This is the beauty of interpretation. You can choose how you feel about the end. But it must be an informed choice!

Text

Yes, text is always important. Here are a few things to consider in this Lied. What colors and words does the text suggest for the three verses? Verse one sounds like a trout that is simply being a trout, darting back and forth while observed by the poet/singer/narrator. Verse two introduces the fisherman with his rod who is looking at the trout "in cold blood." The observer is not concerned because with the clear water, the trout will not fall into the trap set by the fisherman; however, in verse three the fisherman muddies the water, the trout takes the bait and struggles. The observer watches in anger because the trout was deceived, and it all happened so fast.

Look at the descriptive words and let them help you in your storytelling for all the verses.

Verse 1
- *Schoß* (shot): With the initial consonant and the ß (with an /ɔ/ in between) as well as the dotted eighth note, there is the opportunity to make the word onomatopoetic
- *Pfeil* (arrow): Remember Nico Castel's suggestion for pronunciation? Hip flask.

Verse 2
- How does this verse change? What perspective will you take?

Verse 3
- This verse shifts to minor mode and features a lower vocal tessitura. And after two verses of (basically) four measure phrases, there are now two measure phrases with rests at the beginning. This is important information to convey as you sing "But finally the thief could wait no longer."
- The repeated notes of *Er macht das Bächlein tükkisch trübe'* offer an opportunity to use the repetition as a different articulation (*detachée*, for example) or more of a recitative approach perhaps.
- *Zuckte* (jerked) can be sung with onomatopoeia as well, turning the /ckt/ into something of a double /k/.

Application of Part 1.2

There are several sequences of arpeggios that make it important to review Part 1.2 so that poor intonation is not an issue. Identify all the arpeggios and work on them individually so they are secure. The same is true for scales. A Major scale is found in the third measure of the vocal line, starting on the ninth and ending on the fifth. Half steps and whole steps are peppered throughout the Lied. I would suggest marking your music from the outset as a practice copy identifying the arpeggios, scales, half steps and whole steps.

Fauré, *La bonne chanson,* "La lune blanche luit dans les bois"

This cycle of nine *mélodies* with texts by Paul Verlaine is unique in its explosion of joy. In setting his texts, the mute syllables of the French language seem to fall alternately on strong and weak beats, but they always retain the mood and character of the song. This cycle was written during Fauré's second compositional period where the piano took on a more important role. Some of his most glorious work was produced during this time. "La lune blanche luit dans les bois," is about the awakening of love at the exquisite hour in the moonlight. This atmosphere must be cultivated throughout.

Tempo, phrasing and dynamics

The metronome markings are not to be dismissed in this song (or this cycle). Marked by the composer as ♩. = 76, try not to wander too far from that tempo when performing this *mélodie.*

The phrases are clearly delineated with rests, but attention to the punctuation will let you know when the musical line is longer than the individual phrase, so it is essential to count beats to come in correctly. The beginnings of phrases can be a bit tricky.

The dynamics are well marked by the composer and should be observed. The challenge in measures eleven to fourteen is the swell from *piano* to a *forte* in measure thirteen. The *messa di voce* exercise in Part 1.2 and the specifics in the examples will be helpful here. (Many of the other phrases in this *mélodie* will also benefit from those exercises.) Pay special attention in measure 43 to the octave skip while you're say "This is the exquisite hour;" it is important to decrescendo on that octave skip to match the text.

Text and music

Word painting is used in each of the songs in *La bonne chanson.* This *mélodie* begins in F♯ Major. In measure three there is a change to the F-minor seventh chord on the descriptive adjective in the phrase *La lune blanche luit dans les bois* (The white moon shines in the woods). In measure 21, the broken chord in the piano should have a shimmering effect to accompany the words *La silhouette* (the silhouette). In measures 23 through 25, the wind cries in the right hand (in the whole step movement) of the accompaniment during the text *le vent pleure.* This awareness for both singer and pianist is important.

Verses

Even though they are not marked as separate verses, there are three sections in this *mélodie.* The first section ends on the fourteenth measure with *O bien-aimée!* just after we've heard the first full piano melody in Lydian mode.

In section two the piano and voice partner to the idea of "The pond reflects, profound mirror, the silhouette of the black willow, where the wind cries." There is great stillness until the "crying of the wind."

Section three has the vocal line, without rests, until the three measures before the text, "This is the hour exquisite." While the triplets still appear in the accompaniment, beat three omits them. The listener can tell something is up by the change in pattern. The piano also has a consistent melody rather than the more fragmented melodies from sections one and two. This seems to sum up the entire piece. Great breath support and much practice of this third section independently is needed.

Accompaniment

In this *mélodie,* the piano has a light broken-chord accompaniment in a barcarolle rhythm with melodic fragments. Be careful not to get indulgent with the tempo, so keep the triplets even. When melody occurs in the piano, think of it like a duet with the voice. The use of three to four note rising scales is one of Fauré's distinctive features and is used more in the accompaniment than in the vocal line. The arpeggio can also control the modulations in the *mélodie.* The rolled chords at the end should be rolled slowly in keeping with the character of the song.

There are five recurring musical themes in the cycle, *La bonne chanson.* "La lune blanche luit dans les bois," song number three, is the first appearance of one of the themes, which is based on the Lydian mode. The phrase occurs in measures nine through twelve of the song and is presented by the piano.

Bellini, "Vaga luna che inargenti" from *15 Composizioni da camera per canto e pianoforte*

Of all the Italian songs, why did I choose this one? Besides being incredibly beautiful, it is a song that has a lot of potential for multiple purposes for singers. While Bellini opera arias are usually incredibly difficult, his songs offer a simpler singing experience while addressing several issues. This is a strophic song with anonymous poetry and a modest accompaniment that highlights the voice in every way. It is also about unrequited love (as all the songs in this group are) so you can play with the nuances around that topic.

Line and legato

The long flowing vocal lines of "Vaga luna" make this is a great place to work on musical line and legato. I would encourage singing on your favorite vowel to get the sense of the flow of the music. Part 1.6 *Vowels, Vocal Colors and Expressivity,* addresses legato and line, as does Part 1.7 *Learning To Keep Your Sound Consisten*t. There are many practice tools in both of those sections.

While you are working on the vocal line, concurrently work on the text. These vowels are liquid gold and with proper Italian pronunciation will supplement the legato and line work you are doing with your voice. There are a few tricky combinations that need extra attention, such as the phrase, *Ed inspir**i, E**d inspir**i a**gl**i e**lementi.* Work on the vowel combinations for the words that share an eighth note, in bold above. These should be practiced until they feel like vegetables for your voice. Practice speaking the text, line by line once you've mastered the vowel combinations, working towards the fluency of an Italian speaker. Listen to movies or news in Italian to hear the flow of a native speaker. I caution you against popping any of the Italian consonants. That is like waving an American flag in your vocal presentation. Remember you are trying to sound like you are from the country whose language you are singing in. Referring to Part 2.1 is recommended for this sort of work.

Key

This is always an important question: what key should I sing this song in? Well, in my Ricordi edition, it is in the key of A♭ major. In my opinion, this is the perfect song to sing up a half step or a whole step as well as to sing down a half step or a whole step. Why? Because it will tell you a lot about your voice, your passaggio, and your technique. When performing the song, sing in the key most comfortable for you. But in practice, play around with the different keys one phrase at a time. And, without getting into teacher talk, which I firmly believe belongs with the teacher, this will help you with the middle part of your voice.

Note of caution

Unlike the Fauré *mélodie* there is more flexibility in this song. It should not be sung with a strict tempo throughout. I love that these days we can find just about anything on the internet. Go to YouTube and find Luciano Pavarotti and John Wustman performing this delightful song. (There's one from Paris in 1985.) It is an excellent example of the line and legato that everyone strives for.

Part 3.9

How to Approach a New Piece

If you are like most people, once you start working on a song, aria, or role that is new to you, you want to sing it repeatedly, but it is better to slow the process down so that in your first weeks of practice you don't practice-in mistakes that create more work for you. You want everything to be productive; singing through a song or aria requires juggling multiple balls at once—practice with one ball at a time.

Learning a piece of music that is new to you

It would be cruel to insist that you not sing it through once, so have fun. Enjoy it, but sing it through only once and then create a practice plan for success. Everyone's plan will look different, but the point is to have a plan. Here is a sample of what a plan looks like

Week 1

- Sing through it (gleefully) once.
- Translate all the text using the template in the Appendix.
- Identify what you are facing and create a list so that you can practice one thing at a time.
- Look at the musical demands of the piece and refer to the Five Daily Exercises to see what you can use to reinforce your learning. For example, if there is a trill, you will want to practice the trill exercise on the pitches in the piece.
- Practice the rhythms on a neutral syllable so they are clear, and you understand how they fit together. Particularly pesky parts are triplets (especially when the accompaniment has a duple rhythm) and the dotted eighth note/sixteenth note rhythm (remember that composers had choices and if they really wanted a swingy triplet, they would have written it that way).
- Practice the text as poetry.
- Practice the text in rhythm (using a metronome from slow to fast). Be sure you can speak the text in rhythm without mistakes. If you keep stumbling, you are going too fast.
- Mark the dynamics and anything else you need to be sure to integrate.
- Look at the melody line and give yourself prompts such as:
    - These two measures are arpeggios.
    - This line requires a very big, secure breath.
    - Watch the meter change here.
    - The articulation changes to staccato here.
- Practice about eight measures of the melody at a time on your best vowel. By the end of the week, you can have done this throughout your aria unless it is something ridiculously long like Zerbinetta's aria, Anne Trulove's aria, or a bel canto scena.
    - What does your voice want to do?
    - What do you hear your teacher saying in your head?
    - How is your intonation? Are you singing in the center of the pitch?
    - Record your practice so that you can make sure you are truly doing what you think you are doing.
- Keep referring to your *Five Daily Exercises* to help you.
- Listen to three of your ten recordings

Week 2

- Review your list and determine what makes sense to practice this week
- Sing through it (recording to see your progress)
- Internalize the text using some of the exercises in the book
    - Deepen your understanding of the text
    - Continue reading out loud as poetry or a story
- Continue speaking in rhythm for accuracy (making sure you attend to all the linguistic nuances that are needed)
- Sing the melody line on your best vowel and work to increase the musicality of what you are doing
- Compare the melody to the text. What was the composer's intent writing this melody/articulation/tempo to this text?
- Work on the spots you've identified as needing specific attention
- Listen to three more of your ten recordings

You get the idea. By the fourth week, you should have a good handle on the piece, and you should have practiced in the best way possible to sing the piece with correct words, rhythms, and pitches, all while making it musical. Your skills should become more efficient over time, enabling you to shorten this whole learning period to a week or less.

Learning a piece of music that is newly written, or recently written

This involves all the same steps as indicated above, except that you usually do not have the benefit of ten recordings and your musical team may be learning the music at the same time. Don't despair; an experienced coach can be very helpful even if they don't already know the new piece, as they know how to tackle new work.

Sometimes you are required to work a very difficult vocal line into your voice that is not intuitive. This is when you must look at the vocal line all by itself without the accompaniment. What is it doing? In the absence of the accompaniment, you might discover that the first two measures have an F major feel to them. Let the F-major chord help you, even if it is not in the accompaniment. There may be arpeggios. Note that and work on them. (In repertoire arpeggios rarely begin on the root, so going back to the Five Daily Exercises will be helpful.) There might be half steps and whole steps that you can identify, and, likely, parts of a scale, whether fast or slow. So, in deconstructing the melody line, you will see that, like all music, it is full of half steps, whole steps, and skips (which are all part of some arpeggio, especially with the seventh and ninth added). It is suddenly attainable because you understand the mechanics of how it is put together. And, like any music, once you have achieved all that is on the written page, you need to lift the music off the page and make it your own.

Part 3.10

Finale

Dear singers: There are so many tools in this book that can help you throughout your singing career, but teachers and coaches also can review this information and offer suggestions to their students.

Choose the tools that are right for you at this moment in time. Review the book every year, every semester, or every month to see what else you can do to enhance your practice time.

Are you in great voice today? Terrific. Focus on the exercises in Part 1.

Are you too tired to sing today? No problem. Focus on the exercises in Part 2.

In transport via car, train, bus, or airplane? Great. Part 2 is for you. (Or re-reading the book!)

Do you need tangible examples of how to put things together? Excellent. Turn to Part 3.

My goal is for this to be a resource that you read then return to time and time again. It is your toolbox that you can dig into for your entire life. Yes, a lifelong study that is useful each time you learn a new piece or revisit a piece that is an old friend. It doesn't matter whether you are a freshman in college, have completed several young artist programs or are several years into a successful career. It doesn't matter if your chosen career path is as an opera singer, a choral singer, a music teacher, or a hobby musician. The exercises and ideas will help you learn to be more detailed and efficient with your time and in your practice and will show you multiple ways to get results in your repertoire that make you proud. We are lucky to be musicians. You are lucky to be singers.

I wish you years of enjoyable practicing and meaningful music making.

Appendices

Appendix I

Template for a Practice Plan

Plan your practice for the week (at least an overview of time and what you hope to accomplish). However, you should amend daily if you have more or less time to practice or if something you worked on needs varying attention. This is a changeable document meant to support you and your hard work.

Break into achievable time segments. For some singers and some exercises, it might be five to fifteen minutes. For others, 30 minutes or more.

There are many online templates to purchase or download as well. See what works for you.

Your practice plan should include the following information:

- Goals for the week
- Goals for the day
- Warm up and technical exercises
- Five Daily Exercises
- Detail Work/Priorities
    - Cite specific examples
- Repertoire Run Through
    - Practicing the performance
    - Reviewing how the piece holds up as a whole
- Language Work
    - Translating
    - Diction work
    - IPA
    - Reading the text out loud for native inflection
- Listening
- Information about if the goals were met or not (and how that will inform your next day's practice
    - Plan versus actual
    - Thoughts about reasons (physical, emotional, environmental)
- Comments
    - What worked and what didn't
    - Thoughts for the coming day

MY PRACTICE PLAN
Sample

WEEK: February 7–13, 2022

Overall goals for the week

- Polish the Cipullo aria (to sing next week in studio class)
- Translate the Strauss set so I can begin working on it next week
- Work on the sixteenth note phrases in the Mozart for clarity
  - Rhythm work
  - Small groupings
  - Tempo
- Improve the Italian in the Bellini
- Start work on the Massenet

Date: Monday, February 7

Practice times allotted and action plan:

- 10:30–11:30
  - Warm up and Technical Issues: 35 minutes
    - Warm up: 20 minutes
    - Work on technical concept from last lesson: fifteen minutes
  - Five Daily Exercises: Note for the day (F_5), vowel for the day /o/: five minutes
  - Daily work/priorities: 20 minutes
    - Sixteenth notes in the Mozart: ten minutes
      - Try the rhythm work
  - Massenet, tough spots identified last week: ten minutes
- 2:00–3:15
  - Daily work/priorities: fifteen minutes
    - Mozart sixteenth notes in small groupings
  - Repertoire run through: fifteen minutes
    - Run the Cipullo, record and listen for assessment afterwards (use the audio/video accompaniment)
  - Work on the first section of the Massenet, breaking it down into spoken language, language in rhythm (slow with metronome), singing on an /o/: 30 minutes
  - Sing the section of the Mozart with the sixteenth notes at a medium tempo to assess how it feels: five minutes
  - Record the Mozart sixteenths at a faster tempo and listen for progress or challenges: ten minutes
- 5:00–6:00
  - Work on the Strauss translation: 30 minutes
  - Listen to the Strauss set for the music that I've translated: five minutes
  - Work on the Italian in the Bellini: 25 minutes
    - First section for native cadence: fifteen minutes

        - Second section work slowly on the vowel clusters for clarity: ten minutes

- Plan versus actual
    - I still need time on the Mozart sixteenth notes that I was too tired to finish during the last fifteen minutes of the 2:00–3:15 slot. Consider using one hour for singing and fifteen minutes for non-singing activities.
    - I was interrupted at 5:45 so need to reschedule the rest of the Bellini work for tomorrow
    - On the bright side, after rehearsal this evening, I listened to several recordings of the Massenet and am super excited to really dive into this aria
- Comments
    - Morning practice was very productive. I seem to get my best, most focused work done then.
    - One hour of singing at a time seems to be it for me
    - I need to remember to hydrate more during the day. I can feel it in my afternoon singing

Appendix II

Translation Templates

Format 1

The first line of the aria
The character's name
The opera from which the aria is excerpted
The composer of the opera

1. Original language
2. Word by word translation (with multiple options for each word)
3. Transliteration
4. How you would say it in colloquial English

EXAMPLE:

1. Hai	gia	vinta	la	causa.	Cosa	sento?
2. You have	already	won beaten defeated overcome	the	cause. reason motive case	What	I hear?

3) You have already won the cause. What do I hear?

4. What do you mean, you've already won the case? (OR) What am I hearing? "You've already won the case?"

Things to consider:

- If there is more than one word in the dictionary, please put down all (or most) choices.
- Resources, such as Nico Castel's books are a good reference ONCE you've translated each word.
- Be sure that each translated word is aligned underneath the original language word.
- Double space or triple space after each line grouping on the page, as indicated above.
- Translate each word. Don't skip the small words.
- Remember to use pronouns for all verbs.

Format 2

The first line of the aria
The character's name
The opera from which the aria is excerpted
The composer of the opera

1. Original language
2. Word by word translation (with multiple options for each word)
3. Transliteration
4. How you would say it in colloquial English

1. Hai	gia	vinta	la	causa.	Cosa	sento?
2. You have	already	won beaten defeated overcome	the	cause. reason. motive. case. decision.	What	I hear?
3. You have already won the cause. What do I hear?						
4. What do you mean, you've already won the case? (or) What am I hearing? "You've already won the case."						

Things to consider:

If there is more than one word in the dictionary, please put down all (or most) choices.
Resources, such as Nico Castel's books are a good reference ONCE you've translated each word.
Be sure that each translated word is lined up underneath the original language word.
Double space or triple space after each line grouping on the page, as indicated above.
Translate each word. Don't skip the small words.
Remember to use pronouns for all verbs.

Appendix III

Online Music Making

Several years ago, it would never have occurred to us that we would be making music exclusively online for a period. The Covid pandemic changed that. And since that genie is out of the bottle, I think online music making is here to stay, at least in some form. How terrific for the singer who is away from their resources to be able to zoom in for a lesson or coaching!

One of the things that I realized during the pandemic is that even the best singing artist floundered a bit at music learning once their normal habits were uprooted. For some of the youngest singers, it was apparent that they didn't really know how to tackle their music. Without being able to make music synchronously, new systems were needed. Fortunately, musicians are some of the most creative people in the world, and new ways of working have popped up. For those singers with a pianist in their pod, life continued to be a bit easier for practicing. But those situations were few and far between. I know singers who took accompaniments, piped them through their speaker system outdoors and gave concerts to their neighbors. Singers learned how to sing to a recorded accompaniment track. In fact, the entire Metropolitan Opera National Council auditions for 2021 (which included Fall 2020) were sung to recorded tracks. And by the end of a year, we all realized that audio/video recorded tracks were much better for singers as they could see and anticipate what the pianist was doing for a more successful "collaboration." Soundjack was introduced and brought tears to my eyes when we first used this at Westminster Choir College at Rider University for a quartet rehearsal in Opera Theatre. We were all in separate rooms, linked visually by zoom, linked to sound on the Soundjack platform https://www.soundjack.eu/. And it worked!!! We sang everything we could think of, we were so happy. And we counted and clapped to synchronize audio and audio/video tracks with more than one singer so that the sextet and accompaniment could sound like we were all in one place singing together. We stretched ourselves. We created new paths. We performed. We made music.

Nothing, however, in my opinion, will take the place of making music together. Nothing will take the place of the energy with a live audience.

But, when you are away from your resources and need to work, here are some suggestions for online work with a teacher, vocal coach, drama coach, or language coach.

- There are several strategies for working online that can optimize the situation and the learning process. It is important to send the music in advance. I ask for the music to be sent the day before as an email attachment. That way, I can add it to my forScore library for use. (Check out their website if you are unfamiliar with forScore: https://forscore.co/) A Google Doc or photo of the music is not suitable. Make sure the entire music is on the page (top, bottom, right and left sides). For the best working situation, scan the music with your markings so the coach knows exactly what your intent is.
- You send a recorded segment of your practice to your coach or teacher for their commentary. Their comments can be synchronous or asynchronous.
- Over a zoom platform (or similar)
    - Sing your selection to a recorded accompaniment

        - A video is much preferred to audio only accompaniments as you can see the pianist. A seasoned pianist will breathe where the singer breathes and will help with fermatas and cadenzas by conducting or mouthing the words. It is much superior to the guesswork of silence.
        - Comments are made just like in an in-person coaching
    - Sing your selection a cappella
        - This can be challenging with intonation, rhythm, and tempo
        - Done successfully, it will increase your musicianship
    - Work in great depth on the language
        - Delve deeply into the translation and meaning
        - Work through the translation or translation difficulties you are having
        - Work in detail on the nuances of the language in your repertoire
        - Read the song as a poem, the libretto as a story in the original language
        - Read the song or aria in your own English translation
        - Listen with your coach/teacher to native speakers or singers sourced online and shared on zoom via "screen share"
    - Discuss the opera, your role, the scene
    - Discuss past performance practices and compare to contemporary practices
    - Discuss the original source of the story or poetry
    - Discuss the poet and who (s)he was/is and their writing style
    - Offer self-assessment as to how practice is going—what is working and what is not
    - Review your marked music and make sure it clearly represents your intent
        - The teacher/coach can suggest additional markings that will be helpful for your pianist
    - Discuss repertoire possibilities
    - Discuss potential summer programs or young artist programs
    - Create a timeline for practice
    - Create a syllabus for the next few months to support what the singer wants to accomplish
    - Work on the five practice tools from Part 1, *Everyday Tools for Musical Technique*
    - Determine the best place in your home for lesson/coaching space, if there are options
    - Determine the best place in your home for audition recordings
        - The pre-screening video has been around for a while, but now the stakes are much higher
        - Higher expectation as to protocols and quality of the recording
    - For asynchronous work,
        - Send a practice segment to the coach (fifteen minutes). The coach will then send you fifteen minutes of feedback. This would be for a fee of 30 minutes.
        - Send a full song or aria for review and feedback. Again, the coaching fee would be for the time to listen, review, and offer written or audio/video feedback.

Equipment needed for online coaching

- Two of the following: iPad, tablet, iPhone, android cell phone, laptop, desktop
- External microphone (note that USB and Bluetooth microphones make your device run slower and with more latency or delay)
- Headphones or earbuds

Equipment suggested for online coaching

- Ethernet (provides a more stable internet connection) and adapter
- External microphone that is flat-response, omni-directional
- Wired headphones are best, with open back so you can hear yourself sing
- This list will likely change over the course of time as new technological advancements are rapidly forthcoming

Environment Tips

- Make sure you are in a quiet spot with decent lighting and no ambient noise
- Make sure your technology is adequately charged
- Make sure to turn off all the ringers and other sounds from your technology
- Make sure you are distraction free from pets or people
- Make sure that your background is professionally appropriate

So you see, there is always a way you can work with your team, practice with intent, and make music at the highest level.

Appendix IV

Acting and Drama Resources

Many thanks to these talented and experienced colleagues for sharing their list of "go-to" books on Acting and Drama.

Michelle Eugene: Actor, Acting Coach
Uta Hagen with Haskel Frankel. *Respect for Acting*
Mariana Caldarone and Maggie Lloyd-Williams. *Actions: The Actor's Thesaurus*
E. Katherine Kerr. *Keys: A Simple Guide to Authentic Acting*
Melissa Bruder, Lee Michael Cohn, Madeleine Olnek, Nathaniel Pollack, Robert Previto, and Scott Zigler. *A Practical Handbook for the Actor*
Patsy Rodenburg. *Speaking Shakespeare*

Crystal Manich: Stage and Film Director
Peter Brook, *The Empty Space*
Ute Hagen, *Respect for Acting*
Michael Chekhov, *To the Actor*
Stephen Nachmanovitch, *Free Play*
Elizabeth Gilbert, *Big Magic*
Julia Cameron, *The Artist's Way*

Johnathon Pape: Stage Director & Professor of Opera/Director of Opera Studies (retired) The Boston Conservatory
H. Wesley Balk. *The Complete Singer-Actor: Training for Music Theater*
H. Wesley Balk. *Performing Power: A New Approach for the Singer-Actor*
H. Wesley Balk. *The Radiant Performer: The Spiral Path the Performing Power*
Uta Hagen. *Respect for Acting*
Konstantin Stanislavski. *An Actor Prepares*
Konstantin Stanislavski. *Building a Character*
Konstantin Stanislavski. *Creating a Role*
Sanford Meisner. *Sanford Meisner on Acting*
Stella Adler. *The Art of Acting*
Stella Adler. *The Technique of Acting*

Nova Thomas: Professor Voice, The Shepherd School of Music, Rice University
Teaching-Artist: Santa Fe Opera, Opera Theatre of St. Louis, Utah Opera, Palm Beach Opera
Konstantin Stanislavski. *An Actor Prepares; Building a Character*
Uta Hagen. *Respect for Acting*
Michael Chekhov. *To the Actor*
Robert Cohen. *Acting Power*
Stella Adler. *The Art of Acting*
Wesley Balk. *The Complete Singing Actor*
Sanford Meisner. *Sanford Meisner on Acting*
Larry Moss. *The Intent to Live*
Declan Donnellan. *The Actor and the Target*

Nicholas Wuehrmann: Stage Director, Actor, Singer

Michael Shurtleff. *Audition*

Uta Hagen. *Respect for Acting*

Thomas de Mallet Burgess and Nicholas Skillbeck. *The Singing and Acting Handbook, games and exercises for the performer*

Deepak Chopra. *The Seven Spiritual Laws of Success, a practical guide to the fulfillment of your dreams*

Worksheet

Prepared by **Michelle Eugene**

Character Autobiography (Based on Uta Hagen's Questions)

Begin to add depth and breadth to your knowledge of your character by answering the questions listed below. In determining your answers, utilize the following:

- Information from the libretto (your answers must not conflict with facts about the character presented in the story of the libretto)
- Choices you make based on any information from source material that you find useful (if the libretto was based on a book, or play, sources about the era, etc.)
- Choices you create from your own imagination and inspiration from the musical score

Write your answers in complete sentences in the first person (e.g. I am a princess in the Danish royal family). Writing and thinking in the first person will help you begin to identify WITH and AS the character. Remember, you are looking for information that will inform how you choose to play your character. The more specific you are now, the more this character sketch will help you bring your character to life.

Avoid generalities such as "I am an adult female" or "I am a young male." Give yourself a specific age! Are you a reigning queen, a reluctant mother, a devoted husband, a scorned lover, a fierce warrior?

HINT: Notice which pieces of information differentiate your character from yourself in real life and from the other character(s) in the scene.

For inspiration and greater depth regarding this exercise, look at Uta Hagen's *Respect for Acting,* chapters 22 – 26.

The Questions

1. Who am I? (Write seven to ten sentences including any/all of the following applicable details.)
    a. Full name (to the extent provided in the libretto) and your title (if you have one)
    b. Age
    c. Physical characteristics
    d. Social standing
    e. Occupation
    f. Avocations/interests
    g. Religion

   h. Education
   i. Beliefs/strongly held opinions
   j. Loved ones
   k. Enemies
2. What time is it? (Write two to four sentences including any/all of the following applicable details.)
   a. Century
   b. Decade/year
   c. Season
   d. Day of the week
   e. Hour of the day
   f. Does something specific take place in this season/day/hour? (For example, Mass, a meal, your beloved walks home below your window, etc.)
3. Where am I? (Write two to four sentences including any/all of the following applicable details.)
   a. Country
   b. City/town
   c. Building (if so, room)/outdoor area (if so, type of landscape)
4. What surrounds me? (Write three to five sentences including any/all of the following applicable details.)
   a. Living things/people (spirits, wildlife, animals, plants, weather)
   b. Inanimate objects (meaningful objects, buildings, personal belongings, etc.)
   c. Sounds/smells/atmosphere/energy
5. What are the given circumstances? (Write five to eight sentences including any/all of the following applicable details.)
   a. What relevant events have occurred prior to this scene?
   b. What is happening during this scene?
   c. What might happen in the future because of this sene?
6. What are my relationships? (Write five to eight sentences including any/all of the following applicable details.)
   a. To people
   b. To events
   c. To the surroundings
7. What do I want? (Write five to eight sentences including any/all of the following applicable details.)
   a. What is my deepest and most driving need in the story?
   b. What obstacles are between me and what I want?

Appendix V

Opera Repertoire Resources

It is a common question, "What repertoire should I be working on now?" The answer is never easy. It is one that is answered by talking to your voice teacher first, consulting your coach, and lots of your own research. Several excellent links are provided here to help you in your repertoire selection. Have fun exploring what these amazing people and companies have put together.

New Work

ALT (American Lyric Theater)

https://www.altnyc.org/ The Aria Access Project is a "free hub of downloadable contemporary aria sheet music written by alumni of ALT's Composer Librettist Development Program. The AAP aims to increase awareness of and access to arias by diverse, contemporary American composers and librettists, whose scores remain largely unpublished." Quoted from their website.
https://www.altnyc.org/aap

Project Voce Moderna

A Contemporary Aria Project. From their website: Voce Moderna is a new resource to help connect singers with contemporary opera arias. It is intended to showcase and promote the work of living composers, focusing on works written since 2000.

https://www.projectvocemoderna.com/

United in Opera

The mission of United in Opera is to inspire creativity, provide vital resources, and to mentor musicians so that they may have a better impact on the opera world. They can be accessed through social media.

Here is the FaceBook link: https://www.facebook.com/unitedinopera/

https://docs.google.com/spreadsheets/d/1Pq3VK96iVAX7Ta1WFogaswrpKYMK6EFtZu Evi_gWLWw/edit?usp=sharing

BIPOC Repertoire

BIPOC Voices

(Taken from their website) "BIPOC Voices is a resource to help you program works for solo voice(s) and instruments by composers who are Black, Indigenous, or People of Color." This important website was created in early 2021 and continues its development.

https://morebipocvoices.com/

General Repertoire List

Wolf Trap Opera

Wolf Trap has a long history of posting the arias heard during their extensive audition tour. It is a wonderful resource and can help singers know what is heard most frequently as well as a list of what shows up occasionally. It is interesting to see the consistent favorites of singers, and what changes over time. From their website: “During the annual audition tour, WTO gathers data on the frequency with which individual arias are offered by the singers applying and auditioning for the program.” Links are provided to the data for each voice category in each audition season beginning in 2012. The project was started by Kim Pensinger Witman, former Vice President of Opera and Classical Programming. As a vocal coach, she began the list because, as a coach, she wished a resource like this existed. Current Vice President of Opera and Classical Programming, Lee Anne Myslewski, has continued the practice.

https://opera.wolftrap.org/audition-resources/

Appendix VI

Additional Musical Resources

Tips for Memorization from United in Opera

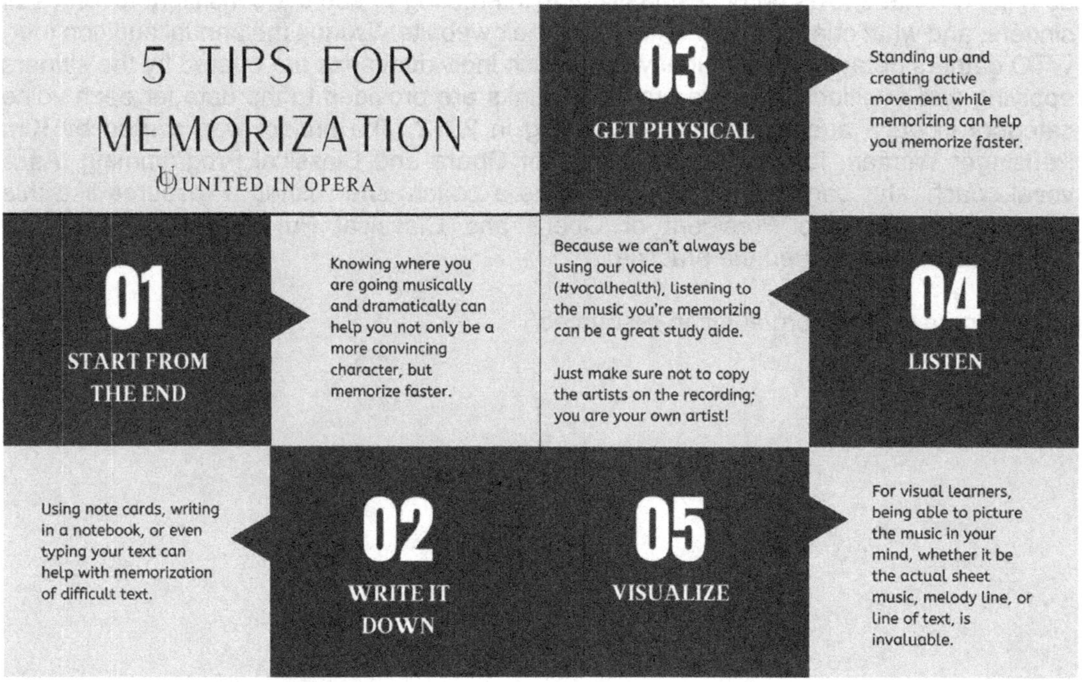

Role Checklist from United in Opera

ROLE CHECKLIST

UNITED IN OPERA

SCENE/ARIA	TEXT	MUSIC	CHAR.	MEMORY
	○	○	○	○
	○	○	○	○
	○	○	○	○
	○	○	○	○
	○	○	○	○
	○	○	○	○
	○	○	○	○
	○	○	○	○
	○	○	○	○
	○	○	○	○
	○	○	○	○
	○	○	○	○

NOTES

Appendix VII

Singer Testimonials

Lindsay Kate Brown, Professional Opera Singer

I had the privilege of having private coachings with Susan while I completed my masters at SUNY Binghamton, and she continues to be one of my mentors to this day. Susan's vast array of experiences in the opera world enable her to work with her coaching students on many facets of music and music learning. From singing recitatives, to creating my 'Yes Book', to understanding the music learning process, Susan has helped me find my way. I recommend her book wholeheartedly!

Brandon Cedel, International Opera Singer

As a student at the Curtis Institute of Music I was given the opportunity to work with many coaches. One of the coaches that I found most beneficial was Susan Ashbaker. I found her approach to coaching incredibly informative and unique. She gave me tools throughout our time together that have shaped the way I learn music and practice today. She would find details in the music that didn't bog me down but made the music more approachable. What I found unique about Susan's coaching style was her ability to pay close attention to the detail of the music and still cause an infectious love of the music itself. She catered her approach to my needs. I grew up playing the piano and would often make parallels between the two art forms that helped bridge the gap for me. After sessions with Susan, I walked away not only with tools to better myself as an artist but also with a desire to want to be the best singer I can be.

Mary Fetterman, Senior Voice Performance Major

Throughout my vocal studies, Professor Susan Ashbaker has been my most constructive, encouraging, productive, and inspiring mentor. I use her advice in every aspect of my singing life. One thing I love most about working with Professor Ashbaker is her emphasis on the ability to musically improve without the need to physically sing. Even on vocal rest days, her non-musical tools keep me actively working toward becoming a better musician. Her musical exercises, daily practice routines, and musicianship-building techniques have been immensely helpful, adaptable, and applicable to all my repertoire. Because of her methods, I can sing my most challenging repertoire without interfering with the work of my voice teacher. Having access to her toolbox of singing methods is a blissful gift and I know I will use them throughout my singing career!

Harrison Heard, Emerging Artist, Post-Graduate

I met Susan Ashbaker while finishing school and she has been an incredible mentor. Her guidance on how to practice is the most invaluable lesson I have learned as a developing singer and young voice teacher. Her preparation tips of separating and practicing segments of music in its component parts and her daily exercises for singers have both become key elements of my personal daily practice and conducive tools for the continued development of my students. They have helped me refine my practice and teaching into an efficient and effective routine that has yielded wonderful results. The tools that Susan Ashbaker has introduced to me have been helpful for both beginner students and those who are more experienced with music! I highly recommend everyone incorporate these practice tools into their musical life.

Bryan McClary, Graduate Student Voice Performance

I have never left a rehearsal or coaching without learning something. You never cease to surprise me. When I'm having an issue, you just look through your toolbox of methods and pull out the right tool to help me get better. I know my toolbox has gotten a lot fuller since I met you. I will have TBS (Think, Breathe, Sing) written on the top of my sheet music forever. By the way, those recitative tips and tricks will become my bible in terms of how to learn any type of recit. Not to mention your method on how to learn newer music is a lifesaver. It's such a simple method, but it makes a world of difference when learning a piece. I'm probably going to have to copy all the works sheets you've given me because I will use them forever! I will never know how I lived without your 5 exercises for singers, I now know why you give these out to your singers. You are 100% right, I don't know why we as singers don't have exercises that help us with our intonation, and aural skills. It has been so helpful for me to use these exercises.

Rinat Shaham, International Opera Singer

Since I began my studies at The Curtis Institute of Music in 1992, I have worked with Susan in several areas. At Curtis, where I received both my Bachelor of Music and Master of Music degrees, I coached regularly with her. Additionally, she hired me at the Opera Company of Philadelphia; as Zerlina in *Don Giovanni,* and as Charlotte in *Werther.* Whether coaching my arias or various roles, playing piano for rehearsals, interacting with world famous singers, conductors, and directors, or offering opportunities to young, emerging singers like myself, it has been clear to me, and all my colleagues that have had benefit of her experience, that she is an asset in the opera world. In my coachings, she always had a positive way of communicating, knew the repertoire, understood the languages, and helped me find ways to practice. She offers a depth of musical knowledge and has a true passion for singers and singing. I will remain grateful to Susan for her expertise in my foundational knowledge, the opportunities she offered to me, and love of learning that she instilled.

Sarah Shafer, International Opera Singer

My first coachings with Susan when I was 17 were both memorable and formative, because she took such a down-to-earth, practical approach to practicing. After hearing me sing, she patiently took me through several practice strategies, focusing on specific elements of my singing needing improvement. She also helped establish for me a logical order in which to practice particular elements when starting a new piece, carefully adding one on top of another. For example, she would have me sing a phrase, but take out the words and sing the phrase all on one vowel, and then take time to identify and work out inconsistencies in breath and resonance before moving on to the next step. Then she would have me add the element of using the vowels of the text, but no consonants, and similarly work out the inconsistencies; then finally add back in the consonants. This systematic approach was invaluable to me as a young singer, and in those first months of school it was Susan who provided me with the tools that I needed to establish effective practice habits for the purpose of improving on my own, without having to rely solely on the opinion of teachers and coaches. I still use Susan's practice order and strategies to this day, and credit her for teaching me how to practice efficiently and effectively. Susan is, in my opinion, the very best kind of teacher because she teaches selflessly, with the goal of eventually not being needed. She gave me the greatest gift a student can receive by teaching me to be my own teacher.

Karen Slack, International Opera Singer

I had the immense opportunity to work with Ms. Ashbaker for 6 years as a student at the Curtis Institute of Music in Philadelphia, and she has been a tremendous influence on my life as an artist. From our very first coaching 24 years ago, she taught me how to learn a full operatic role and gave me my first professional contract at the Opera Company of Philadelphia. The skill of learning how to study an orchestral score and memorization I owe a great deal to Susan. As a young artist she created opportunities for me to perform on the great stage of the Academy of Music. Under her guidance I was awarded an internship to study and cover roles at the Opera Company of Philadelphia. This program created by Ms. Ashbaker was to give students the opportunity to learn major roles, sing with orchestra in the final *sitzprobe* and to be a part of the rehearsal process. Under her leadership, I was able to learn Mimi in Puccini's *La Bohème*, Alice Ford in Verdi's *Falstaff* and Pamina in Mozart's *Die Zauberflöte,* all roles I have had the pleasure to sing on the professional stage. I owe a great deal of my professional success to Susan for always demanding excellence that has carried me quite far in this business. She is a gift to our opera community.

About the Author

Susan Shiplett Ashbaker, Associate Professor and Director of Westminster Opera Theatre for Westminster Choir College at Rider University and Director for the CoOPERAtive Program at Westminster, brings over 40 years of experience in the performing arts. Ms. Ashbaker is active in the opera/vocal world as an independent artistic advisor and consultant, master class presenter, lecturer, and opera/vocal coach. Her experience on both sides of the opera industry gives her a rare and comprehensive approach to key elements of career advancement for singers as well as a unique vantage point in the administration of opera companies, arts organizations, and institutions of higher learning. She is in demand as a master class presenter, having presented recently at Boston Conservatory, University of Miami, Binghamton University, Montclair University, Rutgers University, and Ithaca College.

Ms. Ashbaker was affiliated with Tri-Cities Opera for five years; four as General and Artistic Director, and one as Artistic Director, and "transformed the company in every way imaginable," according to the former Board Chair. Additionally, Ms. Ashbaker served Opera Company of Philadelphia (OCP) for sixteen years, the last eleven as director of artistic and music administration. She led casting practices and reestablished the Company as a pioneer in offering advancements to young singers before they achieved national or international recognition, gave unique opportunities to well-established artists, and supervised all activities of the artistic and music departments. Under her direction, OCP established an intern program with the Curtis Institute of Music.

Ms. Ashbaker has worked as assistant conductor/vocal coach with New York City Opera, European Center for Opera and Vocal Arts, Israeli Vocal Arts Institute, International Vocal Arts Institute in Montreal, *Theater am Goetheplatz* (Bremen, Germany) and Academy of Vocal Arts, and she was on the faculty of the Curtis Institute of Music for nearly 20 years.

A frequent judge for the Metropolitan Opera National Council Auditions and former participant on the MET Quiz Show, Ms. Ashbaker has also participated as panelist with Opera America, New York State Council on the Arts, National Endowment for the Arts, judge for the Jensen Foundation, Marian Anderson Emerging Artist Competition, and the Richard Tucker Foundation Auditions, among others. Ms. Ashbaker trained at Southern Illinois University and *l'École Normale de Musique de Paris* and received a second master's degree in vocal accompanying and coaching from University of Illinois under the tutelage of John Wustman.